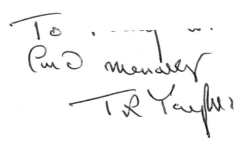

Out of The Silence

Reflections from a Ministry

T Ralph Taylor

This book is for those seeking to spend some
daily time in silent contemplation.
A time of meaningful calm to
help on the journey to a life of peace and harmony.

It is, as always, dedicated to my family,
Irene, Lindsey and Keith,
Ross and Louise.

Also, to the many friends I made during my time as
Parish Minister
In Motherwell Manse Road
Shotts Calderhead
Clackmannan Parish Church

Also, to the members of Group 96 in Rosyth where it all began.
To all of the members of that group and especially Alan, no
longer with us.

Fond memories of
Rev J L Cowie
(known as Ian)

Foreword

This is the third volume from T Ralph Taylor, the first, Tao Te Ching; an Interpretive Translation gave an insightful translation of the work of Lao Tzu and received acclaim as easy to read with interesting thoughts to ponder and meditate. The second, The Tao of Mindfulness, included inspiring words for creative people. In this work Ralph will share his reflections from a ministry, revealing for the reader some insights, at times gained through the practice of meditation, in the form of stories and poems.

In his introduction, Ralph will explain the origins of his study of meditation during a difficult time in his life. I believe Ralph always had a need for solitude and thinking space, taking up as he has always done, solitary pursuits such as long-distance running. He does however also take joy from the company of others. He has formed relationships with an eclectic mix of the people that have crossed his path both professionally and personally on his journey through life. He has at times been accused of what some would call being nosy, although he would rather the term "people watcher", I tend to think of this as an unending curiosity. I believe that the combining of all these traits has allowed Ralph to process and articulate the stories within this volume in a meaningful way, that if engaged with fully as he suggests, in relaxation, with imagination, in silence and with thanks will unlock for the reader the tangle of thoughts and feelings that we all at times encounter.

As Ralph's daughter some of the stories contained with this volume are familiar and yet at the same time unfamiliar. Sometimes a familiar tale may be set in a different time or place and yet suggest the same meaning. At other times it is the reader's time or place that has altered giving the same story a different meaning. This is the skill that my father has, for the telling of a story at the right time and the right place. This collection brought together here has individual stories that will have meaning for the reader at different times and in different places along the journey of life. Use it as Ralph intends, after a read through to gain a feeling for the contents, come back and read again to illicit a deeper meaning at a time and place of your choosing.

Although some of Ralph's stories from a ministry have their origin in Christianity and other religious teachings, no belief in the divine is required to take the meaning and the positive intention with which they are shared. While travelling recently in India a learned friend would recount to me a variety of stories from the Hindu religion. At first as someone lacking in a belief of the divine, I struggled to engage with these. Over time I began to see the deeper meaning and the value of these stories to smooth the path and enhance the journey of life. Likewise, here open your heart and mind and enjoy these stories on whichever level brings you meaning.

Lindsey A Milroy.

Introduction

Having lived a number of years, like many others I have had my high moments and my down times. The highs when things have been going well and everything seems to go as desired. I have also, as have most, had those moments I call, "the dark nights of my inner being," wondering which way to turn and what to do to get myself out of the feeling that nothing I do is going well. Those times when you feel like just giving up and giving in. I have not followed through with this and surrendered to defeat because I have learned to make the inward journey to find again the cornerstone of my life and have listened once again to the still small voice within.

Isaiah puts it this way, "This is my resting place, let the weary rest," or again "This is the place of repose."

Isaiah: 28.

Jesus says,

"Come to me, all you who are weary and burdened, and I will give you rest."

Matthew: 11.

The Buddha said,

"Those who are awake will no longer be afraid of nightmares. Those who have recognised the nature of the rope that seemed to be a serpent will cease to tremble."

The Sermon at Raajmahal.

It is no exaggeration to say that regular times of silent meditation can transform times of despair into new paths of hope. It is not always a comfortable experience because there are times when one has to face up to some honest truths about ourselves. Meditation and silent times of quiet thinking is not some magical panacea that will work overnight. It is worthy of any time spent and any hard thoughts and decisions that are called for because the results are manifold. It brings a sense of contentment and a real awareness of happiness that is seldom found elsewhere.

Some other benefits accrue, such as becoming less critical of others and a less judgemental attitude. I make no promises that it brings a more controlled thinking person. To make that claim I would have to say that I had failed in the process. My mind is as active as ever it has been; it might be more controlled thinking but no less active.

The following pages make no effort to do any deep theological study of biblical texts. What it offers is another way of looking at some of the well-known things that are found in the pages of Christian Scripture, allowing them to speak afresh for you, the reader. No attempt, for example, is made to question whether Jesus put forth his hand and calmed the waves, it merely invites you to experience a sense of real calm from the story.

It is an aid to personal search and insight, and help to a closer understanding of the self.

They have, in the main, come from a time of reflection of my time as Parish Minister. When I left the Ministry, I became a Teacher of Philosophy and World Religions. My growth, understanding, and considering the meaning and purpose of life did not stop or even slow down so there will be some points in this book where I give some insights from other places that have better helped me on my journey.

This is not a manual of fitness, either spiritual or physical. It is merely a collection of what for me have been gems that have brought a sparkle of light to bear. Some facets of the diamond that is my inner thinking.

I offer it humbly and hope it brings some insight as it is read.

A few help notes on how to get the best from the contents of this book.

I have called this book, "Out of the Silence," with a subtitle, "Reflections from a ministry." I spent twenty years as a Church of Scotland Parish Minister. I served in a number of parishes in the central belt of Scotland. During this time, I served as a Prison Chaplain, Hospital Chaplain, School Chaplain and Chaplain in a Steelworks. These reflections, therefore, have grown out of a number of experiences and meetings of people.

I had a time when due to the overuse of my voice I damaged my vocal cords and had three operations and a lengthy period of being unable to speak. At one time there was the possibility of never speaking again. I communicated using pencil and paper and sign language.

During this time of silence, I developed one or two skills. I studied the practice of meditation, I taught myself to paint, my already love of nature deepened, and alongside my theology, I studied many of the eastern philosophies of life.

It follows then that in this book there will be many influences at work. I have spent time making sure that there is not a mix and match that would only end up in confusion, but I have not held back from taking what I have learned over the years from many sources and offered them here in the hope that they bring some insight.

When putting this book together I began with the thought of having three sections: Poems and Thoughts, Meditations and Stories, and Insights. When I sat down to begin, I began to see that this was in many respects a false division. When are a poem and a thought not a meditation? When are stories and thoughts not able to be used as an aid to meditation? I, therefore, decided to write them as they came to me, Out of the Silence, and offer them in this random way.

I have always felt that meditation becomes a very personal thing and the insights gained come from personal experiences. I would not, therefore, advise that there is any one way that this material should be used.

There are some things that over the years I have found valuable and offer them as an aid to be used or ignored.

Whatever part of this book you turn to, or even randomly select, there are four helpful things worthy of attention.

Relax...... Read........ Use Imagination.......Be Silent...... and a fifth possible, be thankful for any insight accrued.

RELAX. I always find it helpful to be completely comfortable. It is seldom the case that anybody is comfortable with legs crossed for example. Make a conscious effort to relax each muscle and part of your being. Take time to tell each limb to be relaxed and feel yourself relaxing that very limb. Follow this little exercise until there is no part of you that feels tense or tight.

READ. Take the selected part of the book and just simply read through it once; reading it at this stage to begin to get a feel for the content into the mind. Then read again, this time pondering and considering exactly what it is you are reading.

USE IMAGINATION. With the aid of the poems, thoughts or passages of meditation try to put yourself into whatever situation the passage is about and allow the material to speak to that small inner voice. Be at one with the characters or actions of the passage.

SILENCE. When you have taken in the complete passage, take a time to be at peace and quiet. Be still and know. Allow what you have just read and been part of to speak to you. Out of the Silence hear that still small voice and what it is directing to you.

THANKS. Try to come away from this time of silence and relaxation with some thoughts or guidance. Be aware that not every passage will give you happy cheerful thoughts, life is just not like that. One of those passages may one day do just that, fill you with an inner joy, another day the same passage may say something entirely different. I never try to force the passage to say what I wish to hear I try to hear what at that moment in time it is saying to me.

Reflections

In the early morning mist,
I felt a stillness in the air.
All in a haze of dreamlike thoughts.
Yet still, and full of peace.
Reflections of water shimmered.
Nondescript and iridescent.
Now we see only as if in a mirror.
Words from ages past repeated themselves,
In the still small voice within.
Here we find a deep and inner calm when we are at one with him.
We may not walk through our tomorrows,
With the answers that we seek.
We may not know just where we're going,
Or the nature of the deed.
But to go this way and be with him,
Is to walk with life's still waters, and travel with the flow.
The day may bring its sorrows.
Might also bring its joys.
Know that all of this is but a pale reflection
Of what around that corner there may yet be.

A PALE REFLECTION.

"Now we see but a poor reflection as in a mirror; then we shall see face to face. Now I know only in part; then I shall know fully, even as I am fully known."

1Cor 13:12

We all have those days when we get out of bed and think of what we have to do during the course of the day. Frequently, there may be something that has to be done that day that does not make the prospect feel good at all. Dwelling upon this is almost the medication for a bad day.

The Cure? Take a quiet moment and picture a scene such as this I am going to word paint.

You are walking in the early morning beside a river gently flowing. You can hear the ripples. There is a mist all around, still and calm. Instead of fretting about what might be, just now allow this picture to fill your mind. Allow the calm of the scene to quieten your inner being.

The early morning mist lets you see everything in a haze as if a pale reflection in a mirror. Instead of trying to see the whole day lying before you see just this beauty.

The truth is this, what you are fretting about may not in fact happen, and if it does this strength you are taking in will be with you and you will manage to get past anything.

The mist in your scene begins to lift and you can now see things more clearly. In the same way see the day ahead, in a clearer light.

We have an amazing ability to see only the worst in every situation. In 1 Cor 13: 12, we are told that we do not always see things as in reality they are.

I had a friend who tells of the time he was conducting a meeting which seemed to be going very well. All of a sudden without saying anything one of the participants got up and left the room. My friend was upset, and his concentration began to wane. She did not seem to be going to return and the more he thought of this the less effective he became in his conduct of the meeting to the extent he brought it to a swift end.

10

On seeing her during the coffee break he had called he asked her if he had said something to upset her. She was a person he held in high regard and most certainly did not wish to upset her. She responded by telling him that she had been enjoying listening to what he had been saying but had remembered she had left the tea urn switched on and had left to put it off. She also said that she did not wish to disturb the other participants so had decided to wait for the break.

We have a great ability to think the worst in many situations. Nobody, other than God, can see what lies before us. Calming the mind at the start of the day and committing the rest of the day to Him we will find an inner strength to face whatever comes our way.

Reflections from A Stool

It was many years ago,
but that night I can recall.
A lonely evening as I sat alone on a tall bar stool;
The room was large and dark, and many mingled near.
Mumbling voices filled my head,
a deafening crescendo of sound
in which no meaning could be found.
Laughing, whispering, the chatter filled my mind
creating an emptiness of dread.
Lost in thought,
of what, or where?
I cannot tell.
From my bowing head the litter-strewn floor I saw.
A face appeared amidst the many throwaways.
A seeming insignificant portrayal,
yet one I could not cast aside.
Features blurred in mindless daze.
Love shone to me from out the haze.
Futile it seemed and yet a lesson taught.
That though in life we seem alone, and no one seems to care.
In every moment black or light.
His presence we can feel, then know again his caring hand,
and be assured he is there.
Christ, the world might throw away, will ever be along your way.
Reaching deep to man's despair,
enveloped in the arms of care.

Thinking of Self, We Pass Him By.

They also will answer, "Lord, when did we see you hungry or thirsty or a stranger, needing clothes sick or in prison, and did not help you?" He will reply, "I tell you the truth, whatever you did not do for one of these, you did not do for me."

Matt 25: 44-45.

In a quiet moment sit and consider your actions.

We are all guilty from time to time, are we not of thinking only of ourselves? We can suffer from a dose of the poor Me's. Hear ourselves saying, "Why does this happen to me?" The more we question ourselves the more strident becomes that inner voice, and the more it does the worse we feel.

From this state, it is a very short step to thinking that the whole world has turned against us. Whispered words we can convince yourself were about ourself. We begin to feel that we are alone and not a single person understands us. They do not seem to even want to try to understand.

Once we have allowed ourselves to reach such depths, we can be tempted to find succour in many ways. We can try to drown our sorrows or eat our way out of despair.

It is now that we need to learn that even here Jesus stands beside us. No matter where you have tried to turn and hide, he has entered with you not stayed standing at the door.

It is very simple to believe that the only place we can meet Jesus the helper and Saviour is in a church. The reality is that he is there wherever we are if we but turn and find him. It may be in the kind words of another person or that gentle touch of encouragement.

How often he is missed not because he is not there but because we have failed to see him. He is there also shining back through the eyes of the person reaching out to and offering help. The more we stretch out the hand of kindness the more we will experience love in our own lives.

He stands at the door and knocks but somebody has to open it to let him in.

My Dog Damon
Of whom the next poem and thought speaks.

Pools of Love

Deep dark pools of umber,
unfathomable love,
forgiving,
unchanging,
unceasing,
Love.

Every move, drawn into the inner depths,
watching,
following,
waiting,
shadowing.
My every motion.

The world left.
They came in, stayed, loyal.
Understanding when oft I did not.
Knowing every unspoken word.
Silently,
wordlessly,
those pools of love,
spoke many things.
In my solitude, I heard of love.

Deep pools of umber,
Love.
The eyes of my companion friend.
the dark, deep,
eyes of my dog.
From them, I heard the still small voice,
that gave me the strength to carry on.

That Inner Voice.

Then a great and powerful wind tore the mountains apart and shattered the rocks before the Lord, but the Lord was not in the wind. After the wind, there was an earthquake, but the Lord was not in the earthquake. After the earthquake came fire, but the Lord was not in the fire. After the fire there came a gentle whisper.

1 Kings 19; 11.

We all at some time or other have those moments when we feel alone, sometimes desperately alone. I do not speak of loneliness, bad as that may be, neither do I speak of aloneness, as terrible as that might be. I speak of that deep inner feeling of helplessness that is almost impossible to describe. I can be there even when surrounded by people yet feel so utterly alone, preoccupied with doubts and uncertainty. The mind is full of questions asking where and when if ever this is going to end. No matter how often we ask ourselves the answer just does not come.

There can be times when you find yourself doing things that would normally keep you fully occupied and at peace with yourself, yet that inner despair still eats away. It is possible to be with friends who you have laughed and joked with in the past and yet still feel like asking yourself, "why am I here?"

It is at such times that we need to listen for that still small voice that speaks above the thunder of the inner earthquake. We have to open ourselves to the gentleness of the spirit, the chi, God, that gentle whisper. It may be shown in the eyes of a friend or as was in my own case the eyes of my dog. It matters not from where it comes it is just that you allow yourself time to calm the questions and instead dwell on the positive.

This still calm voice can come to us in the most unexpected of moments and places. No matter how terrible the circumstances of life may seem that inner voice whispers, this too shall end. This may sound like empty words but in the stillness of a moment consider times from the past when things have seemed so hopeless and yet there comes a new found strength to carry on, from where it came you do not know. Those little moments that have now taken on a deeper sense of purpose.

It is learning to be open for those times and moments, allowing them to come and remove the negative and replace with positive and joyful thoughts.

At one of the lowest moments of my life and career, it was the eyes of my dog that said loud and clear that this was not the end but a new beginning, as it turned out to be. There was once an advertisement that said, "Say it with Flowers." It can be true that in even the smallest of things, even the petals of a dandelion we can hear that still small voice.

We can hear the voice of life, the Lord, amidst the roar of the world when we open our minds to the pulse of creation.

A Letter to Isaiah

Dear Isaiah

Having just finished reading the sixth chapter of your book I could not resist writing this letter to you in the way of seeking some clarification. It is indeed an inspiring chapter, possibly the best one in your complete writing. How I would love to sit down and discuss it with you, there being a few things that leave me questioning.

My first question Isaiah is this: I am wondering how it is when you enter the temple you seem to have those marvellous and moving visions like the one you had in the year that King Uzziah died? In all the years I have been going into the church I have never seemed to have such visions.

I am familiar with the number of pipes that the organ has, but I never come into contact with seraphs or cherubim. I find it all rather difficult to comprehend. I was wondering Isaiah, what kind of frame of mind is it that you have as you enter the temple? Do you enter with sense of expectancy ready to come face to face with your God? Or do you enter expecting the preacher just might on this day entertain me?

I am reminded of the discussion I had one day on the way home from church with some of my fellow Christians, and with one particular family who attended on a regular basis. The old father said, "The minister was very dry today, almost verging on boring." "Yes," responded the mother, "he also went on far too long, there is a good chance that the dinner in the oven will be overcooked. At this point, their young son spoke up, " It was not so bad, I thought it was good value for the fifty pence I put in the offering plate."

I am wondering Isaiah if we went with the same expectations as you would we not end up so disappointed? Seems to me that we do not expect to meet God and therefore we fail to see him there waiting for us.

The next thing that caught my attention was your reaction to the vision. The very first thing that occurred was that looking again at yourself, you seemed to become acutely aware of your own inadequacies. Having looked at yourself you did not like what you saw. "Woe is me!" you cried, "I am ruined! For I am a man of unclean lips." Maybe it is the same for us, Isaiah, we do not like what we see of ourselves, so we play self-righteous building a wall around ourselves, keeping God and pain at arm's length.

Do we need to become a bit more like yourself Isaiah? Do we need to be a bit more honest with ourselves? I suspect it was not easy to admit your failings and weaknesses and it is the same for us, we do not have the desire to become truly honest and face the difficulty of making a fresh beginning so we leave as disappointed as we were when we arrived, with little or no expectations.

It seems that on that day not only did you see yourself for what you were but you also became aware that forgiveness was as you stood before your God. Having found this enlightenment your life took a very sudden change. You heard your God ask a question, "Whom shall I send?" With no hesitation, you responded. "Here I am Lord, send me."

I have to thank you, Isaiah, for this. It never is simple to admit our failings and accept that we need to be forgiven and make a clean break and start afresh. We all know the theory and possibly even the theology yet we continue to beat ourselves and carry the burden of past mistakes onward with us.

Maybe you are right? Maybe we need to follow your example. Like you learn to say, "Yes Lord I am free to start again, here I am, send me."

Some Further Thoughts Isaiah.

Dear Isaiah,

I have been giving some further thoughts after sending you my first letter. I finished discussing. I was thinking further about the idea of accepting forgiveness. It is talked about all the time by so many but look at us, so unlike you who sees the need and accepts. You had a new beginning, the new beginning so many Christians speak about.

The reality is very different. They trudge down to the Church for their time of worship, as I said in my last communication, no expectations almost just going through the process. They make their way there, just as I did, burdened down with the mistakes of the past lying heavily on their shoulders. Get to the door of the church and unlike you, when you arrived at the temple where you took your burdens with you and then deposited them at the door ready to be lifted on the way back out. Plenty of talk about forgiveness being given and received but mostly just theory.

How we need to learn from you, Isaiah. You accepted forgiveness, you offered yourself in service and did not turn your back on the challenge you were given.

You were told to go and preach and teach people who were not going to listen. Not an easy task at all, in fact almost an impossible mission. You did not turn to your God and say, "Wait a minute Lord that is a very difficult thing you are asking me to do." You never for one minute made excuses about your inability to accomplish the task. No, you said, "Here I am, send me."

I think we need to give some serious thought to this Isaiah. We Christians claim to follow Jesus; we say that we have been called to take up the cross and follow him. But the reality is, or so it seems, we will follow as long as the road is not too difficult, the burden not too great. We will take up the cross, as long as it is not to heavy or makes us feel uncomfortable. We will follow until following gets in the way of us doing what it is we really want to be doing. So unlike you Isaiah, a man who said, "Here I am, send me." and never asked about the cost.

You did ask, "For how long?' The reply left you feeling that there was no set time span, it was not a case of go and preach and teach for a short term then retire; no it was to be a lifetime mission. There was to be no compromise of the message either, you were to tell it as it was. There was to be no seeking of popularity, no desire to be loved and lauded, to be a celebrity. It was all about standing up and being counted.

How often have I in my life promised to do what I knew to be the right thing but the moment the going got tough I got going. Not in the direction I had meant to but rather, to the easy way.

I, and I know many others, we see things we do not like. Hear things we do not agree with. Watch as people abuse and walk over others. Act as if the only thing that matters is their happiness and do nothing at all about. I pass by on the other side. Keeping the peace I say, but deep down I know I am shirking the issues for my own peace.

Isaiah, I thank you for those few verses that have challenged me. Your honesty and yet your frailty, your acceptance of the mistakes you have made but the taking in both hands the new beginning being offered. You are indeed an inspiration to me. I hope that I can rise to the challenge to be just like you. May I learn from the example you set and indeed take up the burden and offer myself in service to others.

For this, I know. The offer of forgiveness is real. I am asked to do nothing other than to accept the new beginning on offer. To take whatever talents I have and put them to good use.

I thank you once again Isaiah for the words you have given me and the lessons I have learned.

A Journey of Discovery.

I awoke one morning, and the thought crossed my mind again, as it had done so many times before, "I have had enough of this. Life is all about doing this and doing that, go for this and collect that. All my life I had put up with it, but no more. This older brother of mine he never seems to be ordered about as I seem to be, the time has come for me to take my life into my own hands and to move on.

Who did he think he was anyway? Forever telling me what to do. My father is a good man, I hold no grudges about him. Truth to be told he has always treated me fairly. He made no difference between when it came to birthdays or any other family event, he treated us alike. The trouble lay elsewhere. My father had abrogated responsibility to my elder brother, and he was abusing the responsibility he had been given. I was taking no more. As I said, it was time to move onwards and upwards as they say.

I had thought about it for a very long time, now my mind was settled. There would be no turning back today was the day.

I went to my father and I said to him, "Father give me what is mine, my share of my inheritance so that I can go and seek a life of my own where I make my own decisions."

I can still see his face. You would have thought that I had stabbed him with a knife. The colour drained from his face, for a moment I thought he was about to have a heart attack and die at my feet.

It had never occurred to me that asking him for my inheritance was almost the same as wishing him dead. As I look back now, I can see that, had I seen it that day things might have been different. If I am sincerely honest, I doubt if it would have made any difference. I was suffering from tunnel vision. All I could think of that day was poor me and what I was tired of and what I wanted.

I was very surprised to discover how easy it all really was. Once my father got over his initial shock the argument I had expected to ensue never happened. My father simply went into the house, entered his room and returned with some money which he gave me and wished me well.

An hour or so later I was ready to set off. My father was there, as was my mother. It was very obvious she had been shedding tears. There was no sign of him; my brother it seemed, could not care less whether I was there or leaving. So, I headed off out of the farm gate and began down the road. I had very mixed feelings, sadness at my mother's tears, some regret that I had caused my father some pain, but also a sense of relief that the decision had been made and I was on my way. It had been easier than I had anticipated.

Without looking back, I can remember that sense of excitement as the capital city beckoned me. I was on my way and the hub of life was calling.

Another Day.

It took me three days to get to my destination. The journey, however, was made much easier by the frequent stops I made to quench my thirst and to interact with those I met along the way. I was pleasantly surprised to find so many places of hospitality and wayside taverns.

Eventually, I arrived and found a place to rest my weary head for a few days before making any decisions about what I might do now that I had arrived. I felt no need to be in haste, my father had been generous in his giving. That first evening I fell in with a group of local lads around about my own age. The company was good. We laughed and joked as we drank together into the early hours of the morning. I was not in the least concerned that I was the one that was doing all the buying, I was after all the one with all the money.

The next day I awoke in the early afternoon, with the first of what was to be many sore and painful heads. I had a meal and headed off to explore the city.

I discovered many inns that looked much more exciting than the one I was presently registered to stay in. Some had their little backrooms where more than just drinking and chatting took place. It was possible to sit in one of those and gamble in friendly banter and laughter washing down the dust of the day. This was a new adventure and I was having fun.

The Journey Continues.

In the early hours of the morning, having returned to my inn and sharing a few more drinks with my new-found friends, I retired to my room. It had been a long day. I thought of my father. He had never approved of gambling; he had always considered it something only fools participated in. That night it did not seem like that to me. I had enjoyed an evening in good company, I had not lost a great amount, though I had lost some; it all seemed rather harmless. I convinced myself that I had lost because it was all new to me and once, I became familiar with it all things would change and I would begin to win rather than lose.

A man could easily make a living once they learned the ways and how to determine the odds. That night it seemed like I had maybe found my next and much more relaxed occupation.

There were other backrooms, ones where men could be entertained by the ladies. I had once had a girlfriend in my past life, but this was very different. No talk here about waiting until after marriage vows had been taken. I could see their reasoning that they should be paid, they did after all need to earn a living as I was hoping to do by gambling. They like me had to live. I did not mind paying, they made me feel good, they made me feel like I was somebody. What's more, I had money and could afford to pay.

The day I had arrived at the inn and registered to stay I had put my money in a safe place in my room. I had placed it behind a loose brick in the wall. Each day I had taken out just enough for the days entertainment and just a little extra for the unexpected. I was always thankful I had taken that little extra because I always met somebody in whose company I was happy, and I always ended up spending a that bit more than I had anticipated.

Then one day I had gone to the hole in the wall and to my horror I discovered that there was barely enough left for the nights' enjoyment. I can still remember my horror but also how that had quickly dissipated in the belief that I would be able to win in one of those backroom gambling dens. I also was sure that some of the many friends I had made would be only too eager to help me out.

It was not, however, to be the case. When I could not find the stake money, I could strangely enough not find my friends either. I was broke and alone.

I had to find employment, the time to pay the next instalment for my stay at the inn was approaching. I began enquiring around the place for some job. The only job I could find was one that was not a job that any self-respecting Jew would ever take. There was a job available feeding pigs that nobody seemed to want to do.

I convinced myself it would be short term only until I got myself back on my feet. I was starving and lonely. I had sold all I possessed. The very worst day I can clearly remember. I was so hungry I looked at the food I was feeding to the pigs and thought it looked appetising.

I struggled on. No more gambling, no more friends, living from hand to mouth. There came a day when I awoke and with a deep sense of embarrassment, I came to the conclusion that it was time to admit defeat and eat some humble pie and return to my father. If nothing else he would give me a roof over my head, a job and some food, of this I was sure.

So, a humbled man, I prepared to make the journey home. I walked day and night stopping only for short breaks to rest. Not knowing what sort of reception, I would find, I journeyed on. I spent much time contemplating what I would say to my father, the words I would use to beg his forgiveness. How would I ask him if I could become his hired hand?

As I neared home my inner fears and doubts grew. Then I saw him in the distance. What would I say? How would he react?

He saw me approach and ran towards me throwing his arms around me and hugged me close. I could swear there were tears in his eyes. He called that a great meal should be prepared and that they were to celebrate and honour my return home

It was so good to be home. To feel clean again. I had time to consider all that I had learned. I was full of regret and had vowed to win back friendship with my brother.

How I was going to do that I was not at all sure What I was certain of was that I had been extremely unfair to him in the past. I had been very aware of his shortcomings but not my own. My time away had taught me just how self-centred I had been.

I had no right to have been welcomed back home as I was. And my brother had said just that but he was rebuked by my father who had said to him, "Rejoice, my son, your brother was lost but now he is found." I have to learn to forgive as I have been forgiven and to love as I am loved. I will never until my dying day forget those welcoming open arms as my father ran to meet me.

I hope and long to learn that like him I may be a forgiving person and love others without grudges as I know that I am loved.

The following is most certainly best to be used as a meditation. I have taken a small event from the Bible and written it in such a way that it is now a "Guided Meditation."

Where I have included a number of full stops (..........), I indicate that here is a place where it would be good to take a pause, to allow what has been written to become a picture painted in words to fill the mind.

Along the Beach

You are sitting on a beach in the early hours of the morning. The sun is just beginning to rise above the horizon, its light is touching the tips of the waves making them shimmer like a million little diamonds. You can feel the warmth of the morning sun as it caresses your face, the sand begins to warm beneath your toes and the edges of your feet. There is a gentle breeze, but warming. It is a beautiful peaceful and calm morning. As you sit relaxed and comfortable, feel the peace flow into your inner being. Take a moment to allow this peaceful scene to envelop you and fill you with its calm: -....................

You feel so relaxed, calm and at peace with yourself the world and yourself: - ....

Not far from where you are seated, at the edge of the water two men are casting fishing. You can hear the gentle sound as the nets hit the surface of the water and the sound of the waves as they roll onto the beach nets into the sea. These sounds do not detract from the peace of the moment, rather they enhance, creating an almost orchestral sound: - ....

Even further along the beach, to the left of you, a colourful boat has been dragged up onto the sand. Three men are resting against the boat two others stand beside them. They are all involved in mending the fishing nets that had been used during the nights fishing. It is obvious that they are in the conversation as they work, you can hear the voices even though you cannot make out what is being said. Even the laughter that occasionally bursts forth does not disturb the calm. You watch, allowing the peace once again to fill your being with a deep sense of harmony:- ....

Something catches your eye, a movement making you turn to look to your right. In the distance you see a solitary figure walking slowly along the beach in the direction of the men who are still fishing. From the way he is walking at a slow steady pace and looking around him it is obvious that he, like you, is enjoying this moment. You watch as he draws nearer to the fishermen: - ....

He walks directly towards the two men as they once again cast their nets, almost oblivious of his presence. He stops, they turn and look at him as he looks directly at them. He speaks and you can clearly hear his words, "Come, follow me and I will make you fishers of men." They drop the nets and they fall into the water. You can hear the splash as they fall and are discarded, the waves carrying them to the shore and dragging them back down the beach. The three men move on along the beach passing where you are seated. You watch as they walk towards the boat and the other men: - ....

It all seems so correct as if it were a play being acted out on the stage of life: - ....

Again, you watch: -............ Again, you allow the peace and the calm of the warming morning to touch your inner being: -............

The three reach the other men, who stop what they are doing. It is obvious that the man is again speaking, although this time you cannot hear the words. Two of the men drop what they were doing, turn to their friends and join the man and the other two.:- ....

The four speak to the others and hands are shaken and the five turn to leave. With little if anything being said, they walk up the beach towards you: -..........

You are curious, yet with an inner feeling of warmth and gentleness: -...........

As the five men come very close to you, they, without any instruction from the man, all slow their pace. The four stop. Saying nothing. The man continues walking towards you. As he draws very near to you your eyes meet his. They seem to be smiling as those eyes of his hold and captivate yours: -.........

You look at his face. You seem to sense a strong feeling this man cares about you, there is love in that face. You relax and allow the feeling to wash over you and through you: -..........

The man reaches out and lays a hand on your shoulder: - ....

You feel a warmth flow through you: -..............

He speaks to you: -............. He says: -................?

He takes his hand from your shoulder and the five, again without words moves off, the four following the one.

In the peace of this moment consider the words that were spoken to you in that still small voice within; -..............

Give thanks and leave and prepare to continue your day, taking with you a sense of peace and purpose.

Questions?

Why oh why does the wind blow
and the flowers grow?
Why do trees stand so very tall?
and the rain continually fall?
Why the hurricane,
tornado or earthquake?
Bringing fear and death and more in their wake?
Why does the child die and yet still so small?
Yet the evil person still grows tall?
Questions that constantly fill the head.
Yet answers are never found.
stand in constant dread.
A man upon a tree,
In wonder, we stand and see.
The answers to our questions seek.
Still, no answers come.
If we can but in his life solace find.
The questions disappear and answers in their stead.
In flights of wonder grow,
as daily onward go.
In life's knowledge grow.

Why Oh Why?

"Why is light given, to those in misery and life to the bitter soul, to those that long for death that does not come, who search for it more than hidden treasure, who are filled with gladness and rejoice when they reach the grave? Why is life given to a man whose way is hidden, whom God has hedged in?"

Job 3; 20-23

There are times where life seems very difficult to fathom or to understand. We can feel weighed down and nothing seems to go the way we would wish it to go. It is at such times that like Job in the Old Testament finds himself asking, "Why? Why me Lord? For even the person with what would seem the strongest of faith there are those moments of doubt and uncertainty. Life can just seem to be so unfair when we measure what we have alongside what we see around us.

The rich and wealthy seem to go on getting richer while the poor get ever and ever poorer. The wicked seem to thrive and progress while the righteous persons never seem to prosper at all. It seems that life is indeed very unfair.

The man Job seemed to be one such person. He felt so desolate, so deep in a dark place, and could not understand why. He called out, directing all his pent-up anger towards heaven and God. "A God! Do not speak to me about God. If there is such a God, then this would not happen to me."

How many people of faith have turned their back on a God and on any kind of belief or faith in anything else? Countless numbers have turned their backs and sought meaning and happiness in other sources.

For many, it seems such a terrible thing to allow doubt into their lives and they feel they have no other choice but to turn away. For Job, there seemed to be no answer forthcoming from anywhere. He turned to friends and fellow believers asking for their help; he found none.

There is not a thing wrong with having questions and even doubts and uncertainties about life, religion or faith. It is from such that growth will often come. But there is also much wisdom in the words of the teachers and sages who tell us that there are times when rather than keeping on whipping ourselves and tormenting the brain with questions, we should simply stop and let things be. To let go and let be, and rather than finding answers find that the questions disappear.

Be afraid and know that it is not a crime to fear. Feel grief and know that it is acceptable to grieve. Be angry and know that there is such a thing as righteous anger. All of those reactions are better than turning more and more within ourselves.

We do live in an age when more and more the call goes out to stand on your own two feet. The first priority is to make sure number one is well looked after and to hang with anything else. It is little wonder that in the midst of such that when we feel a time of weakness, we castigate ourselves.

There is nothing wrong with giving help to one another if it is even allowing another to know that we are there for them. Likewise, there is no need to feel that we are an island, It is permissible to share and find strength in another. it takes a brave person to admit that like Job we are feeling defeated. At such times it may be faith that restores or it may be simply finding that inner strength that we have if we but allow it to surface and strengthen us.

John Lennon tells of the time he was asked by a teacher what he wanted to be when he grew up. He thought for a moment and replied that he wanted to be happy. The teacher told him he had not understood the question. He told the teacher she had not understood life.

There are some questions that need to be asked but it was the Buddha who said that there are some answers it is unnecessary to find.

This is another Biblical account told in a new way. Looking afresh at something often helps us to put our fingers on some things that may have been testing us or raising concerns within our minds and bring some clarity.

A Bereft Man

I have often looked back in real desire to try and fathom when my life began to fall apart. It most certainly did go wrong, and I always hoped that if I could spot just when it began, I might be able to understand a little better. Knowing this might help me at a future date to change the course of events.

Until the time I am about to recount for you things had been going very well indeed. Truth to be told they were going much better than just well; things could not really have been much better.

I had lived many happy years with my wife, my seven sons and my three daughters. My sons and daughters were people that my wife and I were very proud of, they were each one of them caring and very thoughtful. Each had their own identities, and each had those little things that could easily have brought discord among the family but they were so unimportant that we had become a loving family in every sense of both of those words.

Together we had managed to build a lucrative business that brought us a good quality of life. We owned a large herd of sheep. We had another herd of oxen and most important of all a good string of well-bred camels. We were fortunate in the reality that money was not something that brought us any concern, we had enough and more for a prosperous life.

I was also respected in the local community, others frequently visited to seek my help and advice. Life was comfortable, and we were doing well for ourselves. I often said, "The Lord has been good to me. Then I have been good and faithful to him."

From an early age, I had learned and kept the Ten Commandments, each and every one of them. Unlike many, I set aside time every day for prayer when I thanked God for the way he had looked after me and mine. I had put my trust in him, and he had not let me down. I said it before, but I repeat it again, "Life was good."

Then it all went wrong. I cannot pin down the day or the moment but it most surely all began and went wrong at a rapid rate. My first loss came when all of my camels were stolen, my herdsmen killed and left lying at the oasis where they had probably gone to water the beasts. Within a very short period of time, it was as if lightning had struck a second time and I found my herdsmen badly burned in the shelter where they had slept. Again there was not a sign of the sheep, all gone just like the camels.

Now if this was not bad enough, we were then attacked by a marauding bunch of Chaldeans, in one attack all of my oxen and the rest of my herders and servants. All gone.

I told myself it could have been much worse; my wife and family were still around me and we could support one another as families do. We would have to work hard to restore our losses, but we had done it before and I was sure we could do it again.

Then the unthinkable happened, my own flesh and blood, seven sons and three daughters and not one of them survived. I could not understand the illness that befell them, but it spared not one of them. To this very day, I can feel the pain of that loss, the heartache as I buried each one of them.

What had I done to deserve all of this? I could think of nothing; I was a good man. "Why Lord, oh why me I cried? Tell me Lord tell me, why me?"

There must have been something I had done wrong some sin I had committed for the Lord to punish me in such a way. I was desolate, bereft, no words could describe my torment.

Surely this must be the end? It was not to be, there was more to come. I began to feel ill my body broke out in terrible sores and boils. It was not only painful it was a terrible sight I had to see. I could hardly look in the glass and see myself.

I became aware of the whispering words between people as I walked along the way. People crossed over to avoid having to speak to me or catch my eye as they passed by.

Then came the final straw, the one that could so easily have broken the camel's back. The one person, who until that day, had stood by my side. The one I had loved and cherished all those many years packed her belongings and returned to the bosom of her family. I was utterly alone, bereft and lost. I had nowhere to turn for help.

I had reached rock bottom. The thought that kept returning to my inner being that filled every waking moment was, Why Lord - Why? I wished I had never been born, and I told the lord this daily and nightly. I wished my mother had never put me to the breast that she had left me abandoned out in the open to die.

I can almost hear you ask, what about the many friends you had? Did none of them come to offer solace or a helping hand? They did come to visit me, at least four of them did, but not one of them seemed to understand my plight, or the depth of my despair. Surely being aware of how much I had loved my family they would understand. It seemed not.

They came, they stood in silence. At first, I thought it was because they understood my pain, that they could feel my hurt. But no. It was because they did not understand, that they stood before me and uttered not a single word.

Then one of them spoke. "Pull yourself together." It felt like a stab in the back, no even worse than that, it was like a knife to my heart.

Pull myself together. How was I supposed to be able to do that? I ask you, how can somebody who has fallen so low ever manage to pull himself together? Did they not understand what I had been through? Then one of them started to ask me what I had done to bring this on myself? How had I displeased God? As if I had not asked myself that very question a million times. It was help I needed, not judgement.

It seemed like the end. There was nowhere and no one who could offer me solace. Again, suicide crossed my mind, but what would my death solve?

It was then that realisation came my way. In my deepest hour, I became aware of something, someone standing with me and within me. Something touched my inner being, gently and silently. I felt a presence as never before. A new strength reached deep within me, a strength flowed through me. There were no words, they seemed unnecessary; this inner burning, this wisdom did not require to be spoken just simply felt.

There were no explanations of why things had reached this point. No comforting words or hurtful questions. What there was, is there are some things in life that cannot be explained or reasoned.

Some things just need silence and quiet. Had my friends said nothing but rather just held me, touched me, been at one with me, this silent wisdom might have been mine earlier.

There is power and a peace that is there no matter the loss or the sorrow. It is there, but it needs to be nurtured and cherished that it might grow, and we might become more aware that we are never on our own.

The Peacock.

Beating the air with fan-like tail,
he strutted,
tail proudly held high.
Each feathery eye shimmering,
catching the watcher's gaze.
Turning this way and that,
rainbow hues dancing in the air.
Splendid beauty, creations wonder. Eye upon eye like an inner
eye,
catching and holding, we pause in awe.
Myriad aigrette gemstones.

Old wives' tales of him are spoken,
Avoid, beware they say,
beware the evil eye.

How can such resplendent beauty evil be?
Surely the hand of creation here we can see.
Much better hear that age-old word,
he speaks of Life,
beyond the grave.
If we were told surprised we would not be,
He stood resplendent on the first ever Easter Day.

Good Luck? - Bad Luck?

For I am convinced that neither death nor life, neither angels nor demons, neither the present nor the future, nor any powers, neither height nor depth, nor anything else in all creation, will be able to separate from the love of God that in Christ Jesus we see.

Romans 8: 38.

I remember as if it were only yesterday the first time I ever came eye to eye with a peacock. I was awestruck by its splendour and beauty. Here I was seeing something that was very special. I was a very young lad at the time and from that moment to this very day, the peacock has held such a fascination that has never waned   or   faltered.

Some years later I had persuaded my father to take me to Pittencrieff Glen where I knew they had a number of peacocks. Pittencrieff Glen and Park were donated to my home town by Andrew Carnegie, the great benefactor. I walked around the extensive grounds keeping my eyes open and my mind alert, I so wanted to once again see a peacock in all its splendour. I was not to be disappointed I caught sight of two that day and one was showing and parading in all its full-blown glory. I was awestruck.

The park keeper had been watching me as I was captured by the bird. He joined me and began to tell me all about the birds and how they attracted a mate by proudly showing off his feathers. I listened intently. He then invited myself and my father into his shed where he presented me with a tail feather from the peacock.

I took it home, eyes aglow and a smile on my face. I felt as though I had been given a gift of the crown jewels; I will never forget that day. As I travelled home on the bus I could see it hanging on my bedroom wall above my bed where I would be able to stare at it from time to time. I had thoughts of trying to paint   a   picture   of   it.

I can remember the utter disappointment when my mother forbade me to take it over the threshold. In no uncertain manner,

I was told that I was not bringing that thing into the house, it was to her a symbol of death. I left it outside and never saw it again, but I have never forgotten that day or that feather.

This was my first introduction to superstition. It was not to be my last. I soon learned all sorts of taboos. It was unlucky to walk under a ladder, to break a mirror was even worse this could bring seven years of misfortune. Never must you put an umbrella fully up in the house and never raise it above your head indoors.

There were good luck events and items. A four-leaf clover, one of nature's rarities, was full of good luck. A horseshoe was full of good luck if you hung it near to your entrance door, but remember always have the ends pointing upwards or the luck runs   out.

I can remember finding a patch of clover on my way home from school and in a week finding a large number of four-leaf ones. A neighbour asked me to take her to where I had found them, it seems you had to find them yourself or it was of no value being given one. She managed to find one and placed it in the pages of her bible. I found this a strange thing to do. My father-in-law was a blacksmith and he could make great horseshoes, but he never seemed any luckier than anybody else I knew.

If I found a peacock feather tomorrow, what would I do with it? I would hang it on my study wall. I walk most days of the week and pass clover patches frequently and have often spotted four-leaf ones. Where are they? Still growing where I left them. I have walked under many ladders and have survived them all.

My peacock taught me that you either trust in a higher power than yourself or you put your trust in superstition, but you certainly should not have both. Jesus taught that tomorrow should be left to itself, not to fret or worry about something that is still not here. Lao Tzu taught that yesterday was gone and tomorrow was yet to be, so live today and make the very best of each   moment   you   have.

Enjoy the peacock in all its glory, but if you see one in a painting from a master be sure there is a deeper meaning.

The Woman at the Well.

It was another blistering hot day, as are most of the days in Samaria. Every day even in the middle of winter the temperature rose as the day went on. As warm as it was there were always things that had to be done and today would be no different. The house had to be cleaned, meals had to be prepared. Then, of course, there was the daily visit to the well, a daily task that could not be avoided.

Now it may sound simple, we had to go to the well, but let me say that it was far from simple. If there was anything that I did not like doing this was that one thing. The pottery vessel in which the water was gathered was of itself a heavy thing, once filled with water it was a very difficult thing to carry on the yoke that was used. There were two of them and they had to be balanced as best as possible, but no matter how balanced they were the yoke still cut into the shoulder blades and the pain in the neck some days was unbearable. I never did understand why this was a woman's task but it was and there was little point in making an issue of it.

It was one of those jobs that every day I hoped would not need to be done, that maybe today there would be no need, it never was the case it had to be done and I loathed it and put it off for as long as possible.

The day I am recalling was no different, again I had put off and put off but still, I had to go. So I had got the yoke and the pots and made my weary way to the well. I did not enjoy the task at all but the one thing that I did enjoy was arriving at the well and filling my drinking mug with the cool refreshing water, taking a long breather and sipping the water, feeling it cool my inner being as it quenched my thirst from the heat of the day. It almost made the toil worthwhile. All the way there the thought of that refreshing drink kept me going, I could almost taste it as I neared the well.

That day as I approached the well, I was aware of somebody seated on the edge of the wall surrounding the well. As I drew nearer, I became aware that it was a man and that he was, in fact, a Jew. I can remember very clearly asking myself just what was he doing there? It was very unusual to see a Jew sitting at the edge of a Samarian well. I thought to myself that he had to be a traveller and being Jewish he most surely was up to no good at a Samarian well. How could he be doing any good? Who goes out in the noonday sun and what brings a Jew to a Samaritan well? Silly really to think this way because I was out in the noonday sun and I was heading towards that self-same well. It never fails to amaze me how when a Samaritan and a Jew meet the old antagonists come to the fore.

Warily I made my way forward, I was not carrying these two heavy jugs and returning empty. I had no choice. As I neared him, he spoke to me, "Will you please give me a drink? I was shocked, I thought that he had a terrible nerve. A Jew talking to a Samaritan this was unheard of. We do not talk to Jews and they do not talk to Samaritans. Yet here he was, asking me and saying please.

I was shocked because he obviously had no drinking vessel with him, and he would be expecting to share mine. I looked at him and his eyes caught mine, I found myself thinking this man seems very gentle, he might, in fact, be a nice person to know. But he was a Jew.

As he looked at me and me back at him I found something very strange happening. I found my heart soften towards him.

He continued to look at me and I heard him speak to me, a Samaritan, and him a Jew. He said, "If you knew the gift of God and who it is that asks you for a drink, you would have asked him and he would have given you living water."

It sent shivers down my spine because I felt sure that I knew exactly what it was that he was saying to me. I knew he was saying something much more profound than my reply gave him credit for. I said rather foolishly, "You have nothing with which to draw water."

As he watched me, I knew he was looking beyond what it was that all other men saw when they looked my way. Those eyes of his were penetrating deep into my inner being, yet I felt no fear of this man neither did I feel in any way anxious. It was as if it was acceptable for this man to know the very inner thinking of my mind as if it was perfectly natural for him to know my very being. Had he asked me to tell him I would have done so of this I am sure.

Again, he spoke to me about living water, water that would remove my thirst forever he spoke about. Again, I foolishly responded on an everyday level even though I knew he was talking to me of something much more profound.

He spoke of my husband and in an instant, I knew that this man saw in me more than the superficial. It was as if I was standing there and he was looking deep into my inner being and there was nothing he could not see.

"I have no husband," I said to him.

"No, but you have had five men and the man you live with now is not your husband." At that moment I felt small and, in some way, inadequate. I had never been concerned about my past before, but in a strange way I was deeply concerned now. I somehow saw that my life had been shallow and almost meaningless, a hollow sham of a life. I had moved from man to man seeking meaning and purpose, and here was this man, this Jew in just a few words touching me in a profoundly deep way. He was telling me that life could not be found chasing from one experience to another.

I thought, "This man is some kind of prophet, some kind of sage." We began to converse; I was talking with a Jew. Nevertheless, it did not for one second feel wrong, it felt right. It was right for me to spend this time with him. We spoke about our differences. He made me aware that it was all so meaningless and petty. We were not supposed to speak with one another, yet we believed in the same God. We could not worship together yet we worshipped the same God.

He painted a picture of how it would be one day. He filled me with a dream. A dream of Jews and Samaritans talking and worshipping together. Gathering in the same building praising the name of the same God. He spoke of all past animosities being laid aside, past hatred being forgotten, people forgiving one another.

,

"Yes," I said, "when the Messiah comes."

He looked at me again, those eyes again seeing deep within me. "I who speak to you, I am He," he said.

I thought deep as I looked at him. I felt that his words were true. He was the teacher we all waited for. Who else but he could see me as I really was and still continue to speak to me as he did? He took my mug and drank and handed it back to me and without a thought I also drank from it.

He rose and turned to walk away. I almost called him back. My heart was full of joy that we had shared that drink. I had given him water. In some deep and meaningful way, he had given me a refreshing taste of what could be. I knew that life for me would never be the same. I knew that I would never make quick judgements of others.

I was sad when I returned home that day as I listened to them speak of the same old things, raising all the same grievances and bitterness. I was saddened to hear them speak badly of others. I found myself asking if there was any hope? Deep inside I knew there was, he had given me a dream that one day could be true.

After all, had we two, a Jew and a Samaritan not spent time together? Had we not shared a cup of refreshing water? Had he not indeed fed me the water of life? Somehow, I had been baptised in the spirit of love of my fellow beings.

The Still Small Voice

You come noiselessly into our lives,
Soundless in the still small voice within.
So we fill you with words,
of our own creating.
Words come tumbling forth
and we cannot hear above the din.
Lost in the midst of growing noise,
we lose the still small voice within.
We create the god for which we yearn,
the feeder of all our desires.
We hear the things we long to hear,
building want on want,
banqueting on selfish appetites.
We take the written words of ages past,
select,
manipulate,
and use.
We make them say just what we wish to hear,
to form a crutch removing fear.
There at our beckoning, discarded at our will.
Oh, still small voice within,
let me listen with my mind,
the beating pulse of silence,
feel that life-giving flow
that I may know,
and hear.
The still small voice within.

The God of Our Creating

When Jesus came to the region of Caesarea Philippi, he asked his disciples, "Who do people say the Son of man is?" They replied, "Some say John the Baptist, others Elijah; and still others Jeremiah or one of the prophets."

Matthew 16: 13-14

For many years, almost from the beginning of time, humans have created the gods of their own desires. The gods of their imaginations that brought answers to the ways of life. The more modern religions have continued to do something very similar but much more subtle and clever. Jesus becomes the first pacifist, crusader, or the greatest ever evangelist, whichever best fits the need of the day.

It is a very short step from this to then claiming that Jesus was a conservative or even a communist. I am sure you have heard such claims being made.

Such language and thinking is a symptom of the closed mind. It comes from those who have fallen into the trap of only hearing exactly what it is they want to hear and to say themselves. We can hear it frequently in the daily concourse of life. The writing and scriptures of world religions are quoted and used to add weight and support to personal arguments. The number of theories and propositions that grow from misuse of holy books goes on to this very day. Selective passages are taken out of context and used to defend and purport many a theory.

Such is the action of those who have arrived and standing on the arrival carpet of life have now closed their minds to anything that does not fit their theory. They have come to the conclusion and the journey of their life stops here. No more are they open to be prompted by the sages and teachers of old unless it supports their stance. No more do they seek counsel in their thinking, it may make them feel uncomfortable.

It is sad, for in so doing they miss the chance of a vibrant and living faith or system of belief. The winds of change go passing by and on their life causes not a ripple. We have the pick and mix religion of, Crutch Christianity, or at its worst, Manipulative Religion.

We need once again to learn as the sages of old to have wide open minds and constructive thinking, not the religion set in the concrete of history. It is so easy to become shrouded in the cobwebs of dead religion if we fail to allow the winds of the inner spirit to daily blow into our lives.

The Winds of the Inner Spirit

Iona Beach

I stood upon a lonely beach,
amidst the beauty of which I was surrounded.
Coeruleum sea stretched out
to kiss the waiting sky.
In the distance, the waves caressed the Dutchman's cap.
Afar they crashed to Fingal's cave
with timpani of sound.
Bare feet, warmed by golden sand,
whispering grass atop the white-faced dunes.
No words will ever express that inner beat
that comes from majesty so rare.
In that lingering moment when time stood still,
so small I felt and yet a part.
Stooping, I took within my palm,
a million grains of sand,
letting them trickle through my outstretched fingers,
reminding me that time moves ever onward,
like the grain of sand that passes through the hourglass of my
life.
Each tiny grain its part does play
to make this vast and wondrous universe.
Each grain and particle to make this stretch of sand.
Each plays its part and takes its place.
I, also have my part to play
to make the greater part.
Creation knows each golden gem,
and for this time knows also me
and does not let me slip
but holds me fast and helps me take my place.

Every Hair is Cared For.

Have you ever felt so alone that you ached inside? Loneliness is something that is often talked about, but to experience it is another matter. There is a world of difference from being alone and suffering loneliness.

Alone it is still possible to feel and experience the beauty of the world around us. Such times of aloneness to experience in silence the wonder of nature, is a life healing thing.

Loneliness is something other, it sees only desolation, it is only aware of that churning feeling that life is not as you would want it to be. It yearns for human touch, for a sharing experience, to have somebody who cares, anybody. Such a feeling does nothing for our inner being or our wellbeing.

It seems far too simple to say to such a person that there is a greater power, a God, energy or force that cares. When the desolation of loneliness fills a life, these words are empty and almost meaningless. They can sound empty, nothing more than just words, the loneliness is neither helped nor stopped by such words.

At such times it is helpful rather than listen to words, rather focus on the many times in life you have been touched by a simple act of kindness. Some would say that it is in such acts that we are touched by something greater than ourselves. It may sound naive and too simple to be true, but it is so often the case that the greatest words of wisdom lie discarded in the scrap heap of experience because they sound too simple.

When we remember the times when we felt at our best, and life was feeling good, you can be sure that somewhere in the midst of all of this there was knowledge of somebody who cared. In counting the blessings of our lives that brought a good and positive feeling about life it is a small step, in whatever way possible, to bring such an act of kindness to another.

The first step to no longer being surrounded by that empty feeling is to become aware of the poverty of the lives of others.

To reach out in whatever way we can to bring some moment of joy to another human being.

We each have a part to play in this great scheme of things. There is no doubt in my mind that we can all in some way or another touch the life of another person and such acts, in turn, bring back many blessings to the giver.

I costs nothing to say hello or to offer a smile.

The Storms of Life

You are in the company of, Jesus and some of the disciples walking along the shores of the Sea of Galilee. It is a beautiful sunny day just the gentlest of breezes, you can feel it caress your face. There is the scent of the sea air and the slightest taste of salt. The conversation is light and good humoured. As you walk, soak in the view, feel the sand beneath your feet. Any cares you may have had, feel them fall away as you walk along the shore..........................

As you progress you see a boat pulled up onto the shore. You watch as some of the disciples begin to push it into the water, as the water reaches knee high, they jump into the front of the boat and grasp hold of the oars lying on the lower deck. You join the two at the back of the boat and help to push it out into the sea. Feel the water as it comes against your legs, you hold onto the side of the boat and pull yourself into it......................

The boat is now fully afloat, everybody is now aboard. One of the disciples sets the sail and one takes charge of the tiller. As the sail rises you can hear the wind as it gathers in the sail and the boat begins to move without the aid of the oars which are pulled aboard...................

You watch as Jesus makes his way to fore of the boat and puts a straw paillasse against the front. He settles down and rests his head. All seems relaxed, and you also feel the pleasure of this moment feeling the gentle movement of the boat as the sails in harmony with the winds moves it gently forward. You can hear the waves along the side of the boat as it glides over the water..................

You feel relaxed and a real sense of pleasure fills your mind. The sun is on your face and you are at one with nature and your companions................

As you look to the fore of the boat you notice that Jesus is now fast asleep in spite of the humorous banter that is passing between the disciples. It is a wonderful carefree feeling you do not have one single care...........

After some time you feel that the boat is now leaning more to the side and picking up speed. The wind gets stronger and the boat leans even more to the starboard side. Huge dark clouds begin to block out the sky...............

The wind from a gentle breeze begins to become a roaring gale, the boat is now very noticeably heaving and rolling in the water..............

There is a flash across the sky followed almost instantly with a thunderous clap of noise..........

The disciples, seasoned sailors, are beginning to show some signs of being concerned and afraid the peaceful scene is no more............

In such a situation you would feel fear............. You can see the fear on the faces of the others......... You are aware of this sense of fear within yourself and you feel utterly helpless, there is nothing, not a single thing you can do.............

You watch as two of the disciples' clamour to the fore of the boat where Jesus still lies sleeping oblivious to all that is going on............ One of them reaches down and puts his hand on his shoulder and shakes him awake........ There sounds like a note of anger as you hear him shout at Jesus, "How can you lie there sleeping do you not care about what happens to us?" You watch and are very aware of your emotions.................

Jesus stands, he turns towards you and looks at each of you in turn. Feel his eyes as they meet yours.................

He turns away and looks forward over the prow of the boat.......... You hear him speak. he says something about being still. You are not at all sure who or what he is talking to............ Are his words directed at you and the disciples?   Are they directed towards the sea and the waves?...............

Jesus turns back; his attention is now directed to the group of you as he speaks. "Why are you so afraid? Have you no faith? What harm will you come to?"............

Almost as suddenly as the storm had arisen it begins to calm......... Jesus walks from the front of the boat to where you are, stops beside you and kneels laying his hand on your shoulder.............

He speaks to you, those eyes penetrate your very being............ "Do not be afraid he says to you."....................

He looks at you again, "What is it that you are afraid of? "...............

In the silence of the moment. Be aware of the fears you have.............. Each of us carries fears with us through life...... Open yourself to those fears even now...........

Be honest with yourself now about the things that make you feel anxious............

Be open with yourself about the fears you hold for tomorrow..............

Consider the fears you have for those you care about.............

As you do this, feel those fears being removed from your inner being, be aware of them being replaced with a gentle feeling of calm................

Allow at the deepest level of your being to hear the words calm your fears and worries........... "be still and know.".......... Fear not tomorrow.......... Let tomorrow take care of itself............. Let go of things that have gone before that are no longer in your control........... Feel the calm of the moment and go with the flow of the day......... As if you were in the gentle rocking boat with the sun on your skin and feel at one with all things..........

Let the inner peace calm your every fibre......... Go in Peace.

Changing Seasons

The last few remaining leaves
hold tenaciously to life.
All around a canopy of gold,
Formed by those that long ago gave up,
let go their hold,
and fell.
Another season passes and winter takes its place.
Moments come and moments go,
life ever onwards moves.
The hands of time are never stationary.
A leaf holds on
as if aware of the value of life.
We too hold on, but ofttimes to the past.
Cling to that which has long gone,
attempting the impossible a static life,
amid the turmoil of daily change.
In doing, we lose that very moment of vitality.
While we look back,
the season changes,
is gone to be no more.
This moment, this now, is but a breath away,
from being gone forever.
Each season has its beauty,
each second has its worth,
to be lived as precious and unique.
When can we learn?
Time is not about duration,
rather the quality of its being.

For Everything a Season

"There is a time for everything, and a season for everything under heaven:
> A time to be born and a time to die,
> a time to plant and a time to uproot,
> a time to weep and a time to laugh,
> a time to mourn and a time to dance."

Eccles: 3

How very easy it is to dwell in the past; to remember the good only the good times. Equally how strange that for so many of us the good times all seem to be in the past, by this very fact the times of this present moment will become the good times of our tomorrows.

Time itself by its very nature is neither good nor bad, rather it is a moment to be lived. There are lessons to be learned from the past, it is the fool that ignores that which has gone before. How much better many of the memories of the past might have been had we taken the time to learn the lessons that were there to be learned. There is a well-known saying that the new broom makes a clean sweep. If we take the new broom to our past we may sweep away the good grain along with the chaff and the lessons that had something to offer lost. The wise person allows the winds of time to separate the good from the bad, but this cannot happen if we are so busy brushing from our thoughts the little niggles and worries that may have had a grain of learning.

Having learned that the past has much to teach and much happiness to offer, there is something sad to meet people who have little to share but memories. Memories are not a bad thing, in fact, there is much happiness in the sharing of times shared and personal experiences. The thing that must not be forgotten is that every moment lived in the past is eating away the moments of the present. We must not let the challenges of the day and life slip away into the attic of yesterday.

One other thing that should be taken into full account is that it is in the cupboards of the past where dwell the resentments which can cripple our tomorrows. Grievances held onto can creep out to haunt our present, eating away at the inner peace and bring on a sense of dis-ease.

Such dis-eases closes the door to new challenges that could be waiting around every bend and every new moment. How much can be lost by holding on to the hurts of the past which stop us either forgiving or forgetting?

There is a good case for remembering the old saying, Let Go and Let Be. In this way, each day can be more exciting than in the past. If we spend too much time discussing our history we will miss the opportunity to create a new exciting history for tomorrow.

At One with Creation

Oh, to join the whale on a silken cruise.
To dance with the dolphin
and sing their songs of clicking joy.
With the skylark soar on wind and breeze
and fill the air with melodious song
comparable with the greatest symphonies
of man's composing.
To run with deer over moor and fell.
Swim upstream with salmon
homeward bound.
See the beauty of gossamer wings of a butterfly.
Dancing in thermals upward flight.
Smell the scent of petals, fragile and glowing.
See rainbows arch across the sky.
Myriad dancing flakes of silent snow.
To feel the beat
at creations heart.
At one with all around.
And feel the inner pulse
enveloped in its peaceful shroud of life.
Humans oftimes bound on paths of ruin,
destructive avenues of death.
Imbalance made in selfish search.
Can creation lead us back
and show again the pastures green
and open Eden's Gate?
That man might once again
bring peace to all creation.
In dominion yet not the dominator,
a fellow worker, not a destroyer.
Maybe then again will earth shout loud,
Amen, so let it be.

Let All Creation Shout Amen

Then I heard what sounded like a great multitude, like roaring
waters and loud peals of thunder, shouting.

Rev: 19: 1-6

On a very personal level, I share some memories. They are very
much a part of my personal journey, but I hope they stimulate
something and even some possible deep consideration.

It all began for me when on my fortieth birthday my daughter
responded to some comment, I had made about people who
went out running or jogging. I said that every person I ever saw
indulging in such pursuits always reminded me of the monks
who, in a desire to get closer to their god, whipped themselves,
or wore hair shirts that aggravated their skin causing great
discomfort. It seemed to me that to do such things in the name of
love or spiritual growth seemed counterproductive.

I watched as joggers pounded the streets in the chase to own
the body beautiful, never a smile on their faces, in fact, it seemed
the very opposite, they looked positively ill as they pounded the
byways huffing and puffing. Here was a new religion,
worshipping their god, that of fitness and beauty. I, in a very
condemnatory fashion, made comments such as. "If they spent
just a bit more time looking after the inner being, they just might,
in fact, find a real beauty that would shine from their whole
being."

Then I took up running and at first, all my worst fears were
confirmed. It was indeed a painful experience, though it did not
have to be. Had I kept myself fit in the body as I had tried to in
my mind things would have been so different.

One day all things came together, the pain disappeared, and I
was running pain-free and positively enjoying it. Then came the
added bonus, I felt at one with the world around me.

One morning I turned a bend in the track to be hit with a scene of
such beauty that I can still in my mind experience it today as I
recall it. There was a bank covered in snowdrops as if covered in

the real thing, it looked as if it had snowed on just that banking. Running around in the flowers were a number of rabbits that looked as though they were being invigorated by the scent of the flowers. In the field, there were sheep with new-born lambs. I felt a sadness in the knowledge that in a few months these same animals would be on dinner plates, but for the moment I was sure that if they could talk to me they would have said that it was a marvellous day and I would have agreed with them.

I am older now and running is a part of my history where it will probably remain. Now I walk in the world of beauty and still feel invigorated and refreshed by it.

There is a wonderful peace and calm that comes to the inner being when we are at one with the creation that can be found nowhere else. It is sad that we are making a seemingly energetic attempt at destroying the very thing that gives us existence. If we could somehow convey to our fellow beings the beauty and health that is there to be found generations yet to be might also find this joy.

For the beating pulse of nature surrounds us and brings us health, vitality and inner peace that comes to us of its own volition and costs us nothing, but our time and understanding.

The West Wind

The west wind blows,
unseen but felt it goes.
Trees bend before its power.
Fields of grass and corn bend this way and that.
Winds of change blow through our lives.
Like the trees, we bend and sway.
Like the wind unseen,
we often bend to wills unseen,
manipulated by forces unknown,
this way and that
to almost daily changing fads.
Trees grasp and hold,
we too must root ourselves secure.
Wind of the spirit blow into me,
renew and strengthen
that I might hold.
To face the many storms of life
that blow my way.

The Winds of Change

"He makes the clouds his chariot and rides the wings of the wind. He makes winds his messengers, flames of fire his servants."

Psalm: 104: 3-4

We all have an ability for getting ourselves into difficult situations that can often take a great amount of effort to extricate ourselves from. I have times in my life when I feel like a walking accident zone, ready for the next mistake. I have met many that seem to carry with them a self-destruct button that they give the occasional push.

I recall a time when I was facing some very difficult situations and took to the hills to try and clear my mind and find a positive outcome. It was a fairly calm day with a gentle breeze, the sun was shining and the hills seemed to shimmer in its glow. As I followed the track upwards, I saw on the summit two trees standing close to each other. Both were bent and leaning as if pointing to the east. From their shape and size, they looked like Hawthorn trees. It was obvious that here on this hill the prevailing wind was a west wind, frequently powerful and often destructive. Yet these two trees held on no matter how hard it had blown. Unlike myself, as I reached the trees I became very aware of the presence of the wind as it tried to blow me from my feet.

Yet these two trees stood bent but firm, firmly grounded and rooted to the spot.

Here is a parody of modern life. We are constantly being persuaded to take up the next life-changing plan. Follow this and your life will be wonderful. A short time later another scheme comes our way and some celebrity tries to persuade us to change yet again.

It is true that life does need some movers and shakers or it would be static and soon become meaningless. That said, we also need to be rooted in something that gives us some sense of security and base of purpose rather than becoming lost and wandering souls.

Some would call this their faith while others, they're inner being. Whatever it is we need to find something in life that keeps us rooted and secure. This sense of a grounding can be our rock in times of difficulty. A solid foundation that gives us support.

A man wandered for years to find the sage he had been told would give him the gift of happiness and purpose. He searched and searched until he, at last, found the one he had sought. When he asked the sage to fulfil his quest, the sage looked at him and smiled, "You come all this way searching for that which will only be found within yourself." We must find and create within ourselves the quiet valleys protected from the winds of every changing notions and ideas. Before rushing this way and that we should secure ourselves firmly with some sense of purpose and meaning that fits our being, not always trying on the garments of others.

A Candle

A candle flickers gently in the breeze,
yet the light holds on as if to tease.
To draw you close, to let you see.
The written words that speak to thee.
The gentle wind caressed my cheek,
like the gentle touch of spirits
to the inner voice does speak.
This little light keeps dark at bay,
it goes not out and with me stays.
Like love, it touches deep within,
and brightens corners seldom seen.
Brings out in us the very best,
and helps us face the greatest test.
It whispers to us I am the light,
I will be with you,
I will not go out.

Light and Dark

Have you ever been afraid of being alone in the dark? I remember summers spent with my grandmother (Gran). She lived in the bottom house in a tenement building with four flights of houses two on each landing. In those days many homes did not have inbuilt toilets. My Gran's was at the end of a passageway that even during the day seemed dark. How I dreaded the thought of going there in the middle of the night or even late at night. It was not really all that far from the front door to the door of the toilet but to me, it seemed like a very long way. I really wanted my Gran to accompany me and wait outside the door to walk me back. There were no lights that could be switched on, so the compromise was that I was given a candle and a candlestick. From the light of this little candle, my fear dissipated. My Gran frequently said to me, "When you see the candlelight remember I am never far from you."

Light has played an important part in almost every world religion, in some more than others. For most, it symbolises the presence of the spirit of God, present and always near.

There will be many who have never had or experienced the fear of the dark in the sense that I have described above because we live in an age where we can get light at the touch of a switch. It is a fact that some people who live in towns have never experienced anything near total darkness and for some, the joy of a starry night is unknown because of the ever-present light pollution we live with.

There is, of course, another kind of darkness that we all at some time or other experience. The darkness and loss that come to us when a loved one dies. Or the darkness that fills our life when a deep and meaningful friendship breaks down. Or that feeling of darkness that overtakes us when we find yourself in a helpless situation where we long to help another and feel helpless to do so.

There is also the most horrible of all darkness that is brought about by the actions of others causing wars and hatred. Or the terrible darkness brought on by famine or earthquakes and such.

We often feel helpless do anything about such horrors and we become aware of another kind of darkness.

Then, for some, the dark night of the soul. When we have lost faith we once had, or the light of life itself seemed to have left us and all we can feel is despair.

It is at such times that it is wise to prepare ourselves. Lighting a candle has always helped me. It takes me back to the happy times and I hear again the voice of my Gran as she tells me the light of the candle is to remind us we are not alone.

To light a candle in the good times of life and in its light to consider again the things that help us to hold on in the bad times. To see again the faces of friends. To remember the lessons learned from loved ones. To feel the inner strength that comes to us from the still small voice within, whether that is the voice of your God or your inner energy, some call it their Chi. Whatever, in the good times, prepare yourself for the times that yet may come. The candlelight speaking words of strength and words of comfort lifting us from dark to light.

This account is told as if we are experiencing through the eyes of one of the disciples. Which of the twelve disciples is not important, it is just seeing it from a different angle that can be found in the pages of the New Testament. I have added the question mark to the title not to be in any way controversial, I am inviting questioning of just what did occur that day.

The Healing of the Demon-Possessed Man?

It had been a very calm and peaceful sail we had experienced across the lake towards Gerasenes. The water had indeed been very calm but there was just enough of a breeze to keep the boat moving. The skill of those who had once been fishermen meant that they could keep the sails full of wind and we made steady progress. It was good to have these moments when we were alone, twelve of us and Jesus, with no interruptions from others.

It seemed that we were constantly surrounded wherever we travelled, each in their own way making demands on the attention of Jesus, and often each of us. It never failed to amaze me how calm Jesus stayed under all of the pressure; we often, on the other hand, got short tempered. At times such as this, we often asked what lay in the future for all of us? When Jesus took the time to give us answers we did not always understand just exactly what he was saying, and we were left bewildered.

It had been a good sail with light-hearted conversations, the sun was bright in the sky but there had been enough breeze to stop it from becoming uncomfortable.

Then everything changed, as we arrived at the shore Jesus hardly had his foot out of the boat when this thing came screaming from the caves, many of which were used as tombs. I say this thing, in fact, we could see it was, in fact, a human being, a man. At first sight, I had thought it was some kind of animal, a frightening enormous animal. My heart was in my mouth and as I looked at the others, they also looked alarmed. The only person unmoved and calm was Jesus.

I felt sure we were about to be attacked. He was like a screaming dervish, as he yelled and screamed, arms flying all over the place. Alongside the noise he was making there was the rattling of the many pieces of chains that had, at one time and another, been placed on his arms and legs. It became plain to see many attempts had been made to restrain him but he had broken free. It was very obvious that this man was possessed in some way, but it was also clear that this was a very strong and dangerous man.

It was not made any easier when he hurtled towards us at great speed. We all looked as if we were making ready for trouble. So, I am sure you can imagine the surprise when he threw himself on the ground in front of Jesus begging him to leave him alone.

He yelled at the top of his voice, "What do you want with me, Jesus Son of the Most High? Swear that you will not torture or torment me."

I looked towards this man and then to Jesus and asked myself who was the most likely to be the torturer?

Jesus turned towards him and said, "Come out of this man, evil spirit!" He then spoke to him again and asked his name. The man responded, "Legion, for we are many." Or something to that effect. It was a very strange almost weird conversation.

He certainly seemed to have the strength of many, but yet he did just look like one very mad man.

There did seem to be some kind of understanding passing between him and Jesus. What happened next was even stranger. Some sort of discussion took place between Jesus and this man.

Now the next thing that happened was either part of this ongoing event or some kind of coincidence, but a herd of pigs came hurtling down a steep bank and straight into the lake we had just left. We all stood mesmerised as we watched them all drown. One minute they were there, the next minute they were not.

I turned from watching this to look again towards the mad man, only to see that he was no longer a mad man. He was sitting as calm as you can imagine holding a conversation with Jesus as if they were long lost friends. It was very difficult to comprehend just what had happened in the last moments.

The events of the day were not yet over. Some of the men who had been in the field with the herd of pigs were running away as fast as their legs would carry them. Whether there had been any connection between the healing of the man and the drowning of the pigs or not, what I was sure of was it was time for us to depart the scene. This feeling was only strengthened when I heard talk of demons and pigs.

Soon almost the total population of the town were there beside us and the place was abuzz with questions. There were those who seemed happy for the man that he had somehow calmed down and seemed very normal. There were those who were more annoyed about what had happened to the pigs and the first noises of us being in some way to be the cause.

We were asked, if not ordered, to leave. I for one thought this sounded like a wise decision and the sooner the better. Some of the locals spoke kindly to us advising us to leave.

We headed towards our boat, which we had so recently left. We clambered aboard and those experts in such matters made ready the sails. Jesus was the last to make a move to climb aboard, he was still conversing with some of the people. As he boarded, the man who had been yelling and screaming quietly asked Jesus if he could join them in the boat. It was very obvious to all that he was pleased to regain his lost sanity. Jesus spoke firmly, "No, you return to your family and share with them what has happened to you."

His head dropped but he did as Jesus had asked him. He set off for home leaving behind his cave. How I would have loved to be there when he entered his home and they saw him. I imagined much celebration in that household that night.

This story can be seen on many levels. It can be viewed as Jesus performing a miracle cure, and there could very well be truth in that belief. It could be seen as an account of Jesus bringing calm and peace to a distraught human being, that of itself is something not to be undermined. There is also the message of the instructions of Jesus, firmly but quietly given, sometimes our first priority is to our families. We must learn where our priorities are.

The following was written at the turning of the year. The year is unimportant but that it was written on New Year's Eve probably is.

Looking Back to the Future

We stand at the turning of a minute.
Just one moment in time.
Yet this moment
like no other
is a point of no return.
Time is ever onward in its flow,
we are very aware of the hands that move.
Aware of the tick of the passage of time.
The past takes on new meaning.
The future holds new hopes.
The sorrows of our yesterdays
become the sadness of our now.
The mistakes haunt us with their hurts and wounds.
The joys touch us briefly,
and we try to catch them once again,
in the whispered memories of the year now gone.
Part of that bundle that we call life,
what will we take
what will we leave?
As we stand at this momentous point,
let us place into the hands of God,
the bundles with their hurts,
the sorrows and the joys.
Let God sift and cast away the chaff,
the joy let us retain.
Now know he waits for us once more
in the tomorrows of our days.
The same yesterday, today and again tomorrow.

Yesterday and Tomorrow

Jesus is the same yesterday and today and forever. Do not be carried away by all kinds of strange teachings. It is good for our hearts to be strengthened by grace, not by ceremonial foods, which are of no value to those that eat them.

Hebrews: 13 8-9

It is a very easy thing to say that the past lies behind us and forgotten, that there is nothing we can do about past mistakes. I am sure we have all heard the words said to us, "Forget it, that is in the past and tomorrow is another day."

But is that in fact the case? Is it so straightforward a thing to put the past behind us?

The past so often comes back to haunt us in the present. So often just when we thought all of those little nagging things from the past were now laid aside some little chance remark made by another brings it all flooding back.

We all make human errors; nobody is beyond making mistakes. We become very conscientious of them and we might make genuine efforts to put them aside and seek to make amends. Apologies are made for any harm or hurt caused and it seems that it is now, in fact, something of the past to be forgotten. Then sometime later, when least expected, something is said, and all the feelings come flooding back and once again you are made to feel those same hurtful feeling as if it was only yesterday.

The past can haunt us and very easily you can relive the painful experience all over again. Sadly, they are often brought back into the light of day many years after they happened and brought out into the open by the very person who has said you were forgiven, and it was a thing of the past.

It is not an easy thing to let go of the past. But it is possible in the spirit of faith to go back with the source of that faith. For many, this will be Jesus Christ, the same yesterday, today and tomorrow. For others, it may be the Chi or energy of life that has been there and is there at all times. If you have such a trust in the stillness and calm of a moment of thought, go back with that being or energy and allow the healing balm of time to be poured out onto that moment as you let it go.

Deal with it in your inner being and let it go. It often helps to make a note of this physically on a sheet of paper and to silently read it as you leave it in the past setting fire to the page and letting it flutter off and out of your life.

No longer is this an internal sore that eats away at the core of your being. It has now been removed by that in which you lay your faith or trust.

The past need not niggle at your present or disrupt and spoil your tomorrow, but it will not happen just by attempting to suppress it deep within. A definite decision to cast it aside has to be taken. Consign it to the past of history and face the day afresh and renewed.

Two Sacrificial Acts

You are part of a g mainly disciples who are with Jesus. They have gathered in Jerusalem and are now entering an upper room of a dwelling place. As you enter there are a group of women waiting to greet you, they have been preparing the room for the celebration of the Passover meal.

Not far from the door of this upper room there is a large bowl of warm water and drying towels made ready for the ritual of the washing of feet. It is the custom for the host to carry out such an act and everybody is looking around to see who on this occasion is to be the host?

There is a hum of voices going around the room as those gathered are wondering just who is going to perform this act.................

You watch as Jesus reaches out and gathers up one of the towels..............

You watch as he drops to his knees and begins to wash the feet of the first of the gathered group..............

One by one they quietly allow him to perform this task...........

You notice that he does not differentiate from males or females or the order in which the task is carried out.......

Eventually, he arrives at Peter one of those who is obviously one of the closest to Jesus in terms of friendship.............

There seems to be some disagreement between Jesus and Peter, and it becomes obvious that he is unhappy about Jesus performing this act for him. At one point he tries to take the towel.........

Jesus insists and washes his feet.............

He then comes to you, and in the same way, washes yours...............

He then gently dries them with one of the towels............

You feel humbled, and yet there is a real sense of feeling that you like the others have been accepted and given this ritual act...........

There is a warm feeling that moves through you as you feel accepted...........

Everybody now moves towards the centre of the room and gathers around a low table with many cushions scattered around it........

Everybody takes a place and all make themselves comfortable ....

There is the sound of happy chatter as all prepare to share this meal............

They are all aware that during this meal there are normally roles played out by some of the participants and they wonder who will play what role.........

Just when you think the meal is to begin one of the women moves over towards Jesus. In her hand, she holds an alabaster jar.............

She breaks it open and the room fills with a strong aroma from what can be seen to be precious ointment........

She pours some of the contents of the jar onto her hands and very gently massages it over the head and face of Jesus...........

She takes his hands in hers and again massages some of the oil into the palms of his hands, you watch in silence..............

Some of the disciples begin to speak rather loudly, complaining that this is a very costly act, not one they should be participating in..............

They murmur about what could have been achieved with the money that such a jar of oil would have cost.......

They could have provided food for all present and more from the local market place.......

Jesus turns his attention to them, gently he tells them, "Be still, this woman will be remembered for this act of kindness."....................

He then says something rather strange; he talks of his death.............

There is a silence that fills the room as each look to him trying to comprehend the meaning of these words..............

In the silence and stillness of this moment think of what she has just done..........

Allow yourself to think to the washing of the feet, see it happening...............

Consider these two sacrificial acts of giving..........

Remember who washed the feet.................

The cost of the ointment and its fragrance.............

Now for a moment consider the wealth of your own life.........

As you contemplate imagine Jesus looking at you and, in the look, asking you to consider what you do with the possessions of your life..........

Ask yourself if in your life you use your talents and your wealth in the way this woman just has.........

As you remember again the washing of feet, hear the words of Jesus about loving your neighbour and also your enemy...........

Consider in the silence if there is some pride or something that holds you back from acting on behalf of others..........

Jesus washed the feet; Mary gave everything she owned..........

All religions, like Christianity, ask us to consider what we do with the things that we own. Some warn us against becoming attached to the things we surround ourselves with. Others remind us that in having wrong attitudes to possessions we can bring pain upon ourselves. Jesus asks us to consider who is our neighbour.

Be Still and Know

We spend our days in a constant rush and hurry,
moving from one thing to another.
Never giving thought to how best it might be done.
We spend our lives in clouds of haste
and it loses all the fun.
There is no time for joy or peace.
From the rising of the sun to the beauty of its setting,
we fail to see the passing hand of time.
Lessons learned of being well
are lost in the hurry of the day.
Through it all, we seldom see,
that we have lost the way.
So take a moment when you can,
and let the inner you catch up.
Find the peace that passes all understanding.
Surround yourself, with Chi or He,
your comforter and guide.
For in our rush,
we may lose our path instead.

Be Still

"Be still and know that I am God. I will be exalted among the nations; I will be exalted in the earth!"

Psalm 46: 10

I would like you to picture a scene that we have probably seen in many films during our youth. Here is the explorer, usually a white man, and with them those who are carrying all the equipment of the explorer. The tents, food and all the camping equipment needed on such journeys. I am sure this is a familiar picture.

In most of those films and tales, it is the white man who is the hero of the tale. It is who teaches the lessons and him who makes all of the decisions.

Let us look at this scene a bit more, maybe all is not as simple as it seems. Maybe the others have something to teach them.

The journey is progressing at a pace and the explorer is pushing things along, keen to get on with things. All at once the rest of the party, without asking or seeking permission, stop and sit down, all the equipment laid aside. There is much of the day still to travel and the explorer is keen to make haste.

No matter how excited he seems to get, the carriers sit still, very quietly saying nothing and not making any effort to take up their loads and progress.

The explorer after much waving of arms and much shouting and pointing turns to the only one of them who can understand what he is saying and asks why the men are refusing to obey and move onward?

The translator looks at him with a puzzled expression and quietly says, "We have been moving a fast pace all day. It is now time to stop and allow our souls to catch up."

Or as the psalmist says, "Be still and know that I am God."

We live our lives at a hectic rate of knots as if there was never a single minute to spare. Is it at all surprising that in this modern age more and more people are suffering from mental illness and burn out?

We all have to take some time to allow our inner being to catch up. To steady our lives, take time out to gather ourselves and our thoughts before making haste yet again.

There is also much to be gained from taking some time to allow the world of beauty around us to once again remind us of the wonder of things beyond ourselves. In all our haste and hurry we are in danger of forgetting that we have a part to play in caring for creation.

In our rush to find life, we are in danger of losing the very things that make life worth living.

Four Good Friends

You are standing in a room full of people. It is a large room with plain white walls. The floor is made of dry beaten dust. There is only one window and it is placed high up on the wall. The sun is streaming in through this window creating a shaft of light.

The room is packed with people and their feet moving around are causing particles of dust to fill the air, they dance like tiny fireflies in the shaft of light. You are standing against the wall furthest from the only door where there are still a large number of people pressing to enter. It is clear from the movement that although the room seems to be packed there are still many more trying to get in through the door.

You look up again at the shaft of light with the dust catching the rays of the sun. The shaft drops down almost into the centre of the room and there in the light as if in a spotlight stands Jesus.

There is still a push of people and the mumbling of many voices..............

Without any prompting, the room falls silent and all eyes turn towards the man Jesus, he begins to speak to the room of onlookers..........

As you listen to his words you hear another sound and your eyes are once again caught by the shaft of sunlight. It seems to be getting bigger and more dust is visible, now falling thickly down through the light.......

It seems to be increasing in size as your eyes are captivated by it. The hole that is allowing the light to cast its ray is becoming larger as you watch........

At first, little by little, it enlarges, more and more of the pan-tiles are being removed and you can begin to see hands working to remove even more........

The tiles are now being removed even faster as the hole enlarges. More hands join in removing the tiles and laying them to the side. More and more light fills the room and more dust is being stirred up by the movement of people and the removal of the tiles........

Soon, everybody is becoming aware of what is happening. Those standing in the middle beside Jesus begin to press back and you can feel yourself being pressed closer into the wall........

Then you see that there are four men on the roof and they are about to lower down into the room what looks like a stretcher. Slowly it drops to the floor almost right at the feet of Jesus. On it lies a man, and it looks obvious to all that he has lain on this stretcher for some time. He is thin and looks very dirty and uncared for..........

He seems helpless to move, he looks up and around at the people, and into the eyes of Jesus.........

Jesus, in turn, looks towards him, this poor pathetic looking man. He speaks to the man......

You listen, as does everybody else as you hear him say, "Your sins are forgiven"...........

There is a noise of complaining voices. They are complaining that this man Jesus has the audacity to offer this man forgiveness of sins. Just who does he think he is? Who has given him the authority to forgive sins?

Jesus looks around the room, he turns looking all around. "Would you rather I would tell this man to get up and walk ?" he says............

Again the mumbling voices get louder...........

Jesus ignores the voices and the complaining and turns his attention once again to the man at his feet lying on a dirty bundle of blankets and sheets..........

You watch and listen, wondering just what is going to happen next?

Jesus says to him, "Get up off your fleapit and walk."............

The man seems astounded but the words of Jesus sound commanding almost condemning. It is obvious they have sunk deep into the mind of the man.........

Slowly, very slowly, but surely he does as told and stands on his feet.........

Equally slowly he begins to walk..........

Those at the door step aside and make way for him as he passes through. He passes without comment or word and leaves, the dirty fleapit of a bed left lying at the feet of Jesus........

Again the mumbling commences..........

You look towards Jesus who stands still and silent watching the man as he walks away and out of the room..........

He looks up towards the ceiling at the four men who had lowered him into the room........

There seems to be a knowing look which passes from them to Jesus and back......

There is a contented look on the face of the four friends. It seems that they knew what this friend of theirs needed and where it would be found..........

All eyes are on Jesus as he looks around the room.......

He moves slowly around the room, stopping here and there in front of this person and that. Quietly words are passing from Jesus to people in the room......

He moves towards you....... and he looks straight into your face. Your eyes meet and you wait knowing that he is going to have something important to say to you................

In the silence of this moment hear as he lays his hand on your shoulder and gently speaks to you..........

Look and listen and in the silence of your inner being hear those healing words you need to hear..........

It matters not who you are, or where you are from, there are for us all moments when in the silence we hear words that can make a difference and lift a burden. Those worries that hold us down can be lifted from us as we listen again to the inner words that are precious to us.

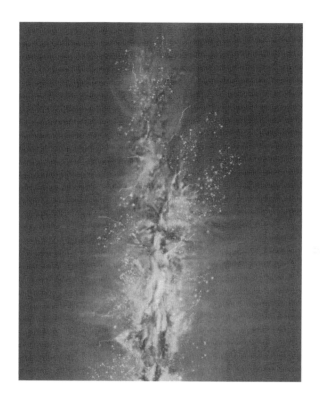

The next few pages contain meditations shorter in nature based on the, "I Am" saying found in the gospel of St John. These sayings seem so very different from any other of the well-known sayings of Jesus. They are very gnostic in nature and hardly seem like the words of Jesus who was a preaching, teaching Jew.

That said, John found that in some way they conveyed the message that he wanted about the life of Jesus. Jesus may well have spoken very similar words to the ones we are going to be looking at. He would have been familiar with the importance of bread and he would have seen shepherds regularly. Other various aspects, vines and such would indeed be familiar to him.

So rather than get involved in the debate about the theology of these sayings I would like us simply to consider them as they are and to contemplate what they say to us in this age about Jesus.

When I became involved in the life of the Church for the very first time, it was to be part of a group of people engaged in writing modern hymns and music. The group was known as Group 96 from Psalm 96, "I will sing a new song to the Lord."

This was a turning point in my life, and one of the very earliest hymns I ever wrote was based around the I Am sayings.

`

I Am the Bread of Life

Jesus said I am the bread of life, he that comes to me shall never hunger. He that believes in me shall never thirst. If any man eats of this bread, he shall live forever, he that comes to me I will never turn away.

John 6: 36-37

I would like you to make a list of the five most important things in your life, at this present moment in time. (If you include your family that will count as one item.)

Hold these five things in your mind. Here are the five most important things for you at this very present moment of time.......

Having decided that these are important to you, consider them for a moment one at a time..........

Now taking time, do not act impulsively, discard the one you consider the easier to let go of............

You now hold in your mind the four most important things you hold dear............

Consider them again and lay aside another. You now have the three dearest things you possess.......

Each section of this meditation gets more difficult as you have probably already realised. From three we must now once again set aside another one of the remaining three.

You are now holding in your mind the two most precious things that you have in life. Of course, I am now going to ask you to choose between those two, setting aside one of the remaining two, leaving you with the one thing you hold most important.

BEHOLD YOUR GOD...........

Taking time to consider what it is that you have held onto as the most precious, the most important. Considering this and giving earnest and serious thought, the question that we can ask now is this, is your life in balance?

All of the chosen items have played their part, family, friends your home all of those things are of course very important in all of our lives. But like most things we find important they are transient and impermanent. Some of them may never have to be discarded but they may be taken from you by the very nature of their being.

What it is that stands as the most important thing in your life can be the very thing that enables you to cope with later loss or sadness at parting. What we hold most precious should be the strength, the rock on which we build a life able to cope with the hard times and occasions of all of our lives.

Nobody ever finds this meditation simple to do. In fact, at times some have argued that the most important thing has got to be the Love of family and friends. Even love holds within it some impermanence. Nothing ever lasts forever except that upon which we build our trust and faith. It is this very thing that, rather than diminish, enhances the value of all the other things which we hold dear to us.

Tragically, this is for some the very thing that is cast aside early on in the course of this meditative exercise.

I Am the True Vine

Jesus said: I am the Vine, you are the branches, live in me and I in you, then you will bear much fruit.

John 15: 5

Imagine a vine growing. It has roots that go down very deep before anything ever appears above the ground. Because of those deep roots the vine seldom needs watering; they seek out nourishment from deep in the soil. Once firmly rooted it reaches up through the ground, frequently very stone-filled ground, yet it manages to find its way to the surface and reaches up towards the sun, the light.

It needs to find support as it grows upward so it sends out tendrils that grip and hold anything it comes into contact with. In this way, the plant can stay upright and spread its branches and leaves, to take strength from the sun.

The wine keeper puts stakes in the field, there are wires running along which the vine is trained and supported. These are important, but long before humans cultivated vines they managed on their own, finding natural holds and sources of nurture.

Once the vine has grown strong, and only then, when it is firmly grafted to the roots and held to the holds it has from its tendrils does it begin to produce the fruit.

We as children similarly hold and grasp to adults to enable us to grow strong and learn to support ourselves. Many of us put our trust in God or Chi, yet how often we let go and drift seeking other things to bring us support and help. Rather than faith in things spiritual we might put our trust in wealth or other people.

It is wise from time to time to take stock and to assess what (or where or how) it is we put our trust? Have we drifted from the spiritual to the material? Or have we decided that we do not need any such support, we can manage to stand on our own two feet.?

The very structures of religion that were put there to enable us to find support can become the very things that detract from what is important in our trust and faith.

The buildings can become more important and drain much of the energy from those who gather within them.

The music and the singing can become more important than the words and the message of the songs.

The members of the congregations or assemblies can become more important than the faith or God that is meant to be at its centre.

Those who call themselves Christian can spend more time propping up the props than ever devoting oneself to the message or the being.

Remember the branches of the vine only require to be damaged or partly broken for the first signs of fatigue. The fruits it bears become smaller and less flavoursome and the vine becomes less value and worth. Eventually, there is no fruit at all.

Once the branch is cut through and is no longer attached to the vine the end is very fast. "It is as well pruned and cast into the fire," says Jesus.

How well secured is your faith, your trust, the meaning of your life? Is it strong and secure or bruised and broken?

I Am the Good Shepherd

Jesus said; I am the Good Shepherd, I know my sheep, and they know me. My sheep hear my voice, I know them and they follow me and I give them life. They shall never perish. Neither shall any man pluck them out of my hand.

John 10: 27-26

It is a very simple picture to conjure up in our minds that of the shepherd with his sheepdog and his herd of sheep. You can easily hold this image in your mind.

We can see the sheepdog running this way and that, hear the shrill whistle and commanding words of the shepherd and watch as the dog obediently does as told. The sheep in their fear of the dog run this way and that, slowly and surely the dog or dogs bring them under control and the shepherd has them where he wants them to be.

But now picture a completely different scene.

A shepherd walks along a dusty track, he is playing a tune on his homemade reed pipe. The music and the bleats of the sheep fill the air. It is, in its own way a symphony of sound. The sheep follow behind the shepherd, there is no dog to herd or push them on; they follow willingly. They know the shepherd, they have put their trust in him and he knows them, each and every one of them.

As you picture the scene another shepherd with his sheep comes from the opposite direction. His sheep, like the first herd, is following in the footsteps of the shepherd. For a moment the sheep mingle together as if they are now one large single herd. The two shepherds stop and pass the time of day. They then continue each in their direction of travel. The sheep separate and each herd follows their shepherd. With just a glance each shepherd will know if any of his sheep are not with his herd, they will be aware if they each have all their animals.

Jesus said that in the same way, he knows his flock each in their own way. Like the shepherd, he is concerned for his sheep; he is concerned for his flock. He has called disciples to be fishers and shepherds of men.

We are not sheep who follow blindly, yet ask yourself in the quiet of the moment how often have you gone chasing after other things thinking that there you will find your peace and your happiness?

The sheep follow their shepherd because it is there that they know they find their safety and security.

What is it you follow? Who is it you follow? To what and whom do you give your trust?

I Am the Light of the World

Jesus said I am the light of the world. He that follows me shall not walk in darkness but shall have the light of life.

John 8: 12

Have you ever gone to stay with friends or gone off to a hotel for a holiday break and found yourself in the middle of the night fumbling about in the dark, simply because you did not know the geography of the room? You were in unfamiliar territory.

Here is a very simple little exercise about just such a situation. You have checked into a hotel and been shown to your room. You have had a long and tiring journey to get there so you freshen up and put your clothes in the wardrobe and drawers. You are looking forward to an evening meal but there is time for a stroll along the town to familiarise yourself to some extent.

You enjoy the stroll it seems like a lovely spot to spend some time. You are once again feeling that it is going to be nice to have a cooked meal that you did not have to cook and served up to you with no clearing up at the end of it. You feel very relaxed. You turn and begin the journey back to the hotel just as the light begins to dim and the street lighting comes on.

As you arrive back at your hotel it is almost dark. You have your meal and collect your key from the desk and head up to your room.

You are feeling tired after the long day of travel and you are ready to relax.

You open the door to your room. Where is that light switch? Not where you thought or had expected it to be. You enter the room in the dark remembering you had noticed a bedside light. What was that you just banged against your leg? You cannot remember the layout of the room. A few more unexpected bumps and knocks and you eventually find the bedside light and manage to switch it on.

The room burst into view with the light from the lamp, everything takes on a new perspective, a new sense of order.

Jesus says, "I am the light of the world."

Without light, we flounder about in the dark trying to find order and meaning in all things and our lives. Often we think we have found the answers only later to be disillusioned. We go it alone and life throws us many bumps, knocks and hardships.

We seek meaning and purpose but seldom find what we seek.

To find something that helps us, to put our trust and faith in something or someone, is like putting on a light. The road ahead looks a lot less frightening. That problem for which there seemed no answer suddenly does not appear so bad.

Where are the dark corners of our lives? We all have them and we all need some help to cast some light upon them. The frightening corners where we need someone to light the way ahead and remove the fear.

Jesus said, "I am the light of the world. he that follows me will not walk in darkness."

I Am the Way the Truth and the Life

Jesus said: I am the way the truth and the life. No man comes to the Father but by me.

John 14: 6

The wind blows up the valley across a field of growing wheat. The wheat bends this way and that as the wind swirls and turns. Clouds crossing the sky hurrying to create shadows that rush across the tops of the standing wheat. Each shadow creates its own pattern. This one like a dragon flying hurriedly past, the next like a ship in full sail across the field.

The wind dries the growing grain. The farmer comes with his harvester and amidst the noise of the machinery, he gathers in the harvest.

The winds of change blow through our lives carrying us this way and that. How often we bend to this whim and that fashion or the next fad to take its hold. An idea catches our imagination and for a while we allow ourselves to be caught up in it. Then along comes another new idea and we go with it for a while.

How easy it is to give religion a whirl to be caught up in the Jesus movement. Until something else comes along that grasps our imagination. We are filled with flashes of enthusiasm and then it dies to be taken over by apathy.

For a time we take our stand and are counted among the members of a cause. We find faith and life seems to be well. Then something happens, often something trivial and we turn our back on the very thing that was bringing some sense and peace to our lives.

We become selective in what we consider to be the truth and what we follow. We consider the truth to be what it is that we want to hear. We even manage to delude ourselves that some of the exaggerations of our lives are truths. How simple it can be to compromise what it was that we had found because it no longer says what we want to hear; or make demands on us that we do not wish to face or stand up and be counted for. It might all become uncomfortable.

We forget that we were part of a rich harvest, claimed by God and Jesus. We live our lives as if they are entirely our own to do with as we must. We have to make decisions but now we leave faith out of the equation. For a while, we felt very much a part of that glorious creation.

But Jesus gently and quietly reminds us that the way to life is found in Him. That the Truth is something that is bigger than us. Life is much bigger and can be much better than just ourselves.

I Am the Resurrection and the Life

Jesus said: I am the resurrection and the life. He that believes in me, though he were dead, shall have life.

John 11: 25

How often have you felt that life had reached a stop, a dead end? There is a problem that you just cannot face, there seems to be no answer and no way forward. You have for one reason or another ended up in a fix and cannot seem to get yourself out of it.

You have tried one thing after another trying to find just one way that will, if not solve the problem, at least make things a bit easier.

This can be a kind of death. Sharing the problem, taking the problem in prayer to the source of your faith can all lead to a resurrection, to a new life. How often the solution that seemed impossible can come in a flash of inspiration. or in the quiet of meditation and thoughtfulness Slowly but surely the answer can come to you and you see a way forward.

There are some who get caught up in addiction, and there are many addictions other than the very obvious. If you find yourself in such a corner it can seem as if there is no way to break the habit. No matter how often you try to break free you keep returning to the same habitual behaviour.

For those in such a predicament, they are facing a sort of death. For them admitting that they are powerless to overcome the addiction, they are beaten. Such an admission can be the first step to the resurrection, to overcoming the problem.

In such a state of helplessness and despair, Jesus says, "I am the resurrection."

If this is the case in life, how much more it is so when we find ourselves having to face up to the reality of death itself. In one way or another, we are all reluctant to face up to the reality of death. Yet it is the one thing we cannot defeat, the inevitable for us all.

Again such fear can be taken from us by handing the fear to our faith to the source of our strength. Death does not need to be a fearful thing, many have faced the inevitable with a sense of confidence. Jesus says, death is not the end but the gateway to a fuller life. He promises to remove the fear with a peace that passes all understanding. Commit the future to the future and live life to the full at the moment. To allow what is yet to be to control our lives is in itself a form of death, and we lose the joy of the moment.

Jesus says, *"I am the resurrection and the life.' Another sage said, "Live life to the full and for the moment go with the flow."*

You Spoke God?

The Lord's Prayer is probably the best known of all prayers, and even those with little or no connection to a church or even a faith. It appears time after time in many films and dramas. How often though is it little more than a repetition of words with little thought behind it? I remember once a terrible moment during an act of worship when I had a memory block. I had led the congregation in the prayer which ended by the congregation joining with me to say the Lord's Prayer. All of a sudden almost halfway through I forgot the next line. I stopped speaking and there was a deathly hush as they waited for me to remember the next line, not one voice rose to help me out. I went back to the first line and the whole congregation joined me. I have often wondered if we had really been praying would this have happened?

Another thing I frequently noticed was that left to their own devices the speed of the prayer would increase. I often had to raise my voice to slow them down. it seemed that little if any, thought lay behind the words.

So let me share again the words of the prayer and then a dialogue follows.

The Lord's Prayer

Our father who is in heaven.
Honoured be your name.
Your Kingdom come.
Your' will be done on earth
as it is in heaven.
Give us this day our daily bread.
And forgive us our sins,
as we forgive those who have sinned against us.
Lead us not into temptation.
But deliver us from evil.
For yours is the glory forever.
Amen.

Our Father who is in heaven.

Yes, what can I do?

Do not interrupt me please I am praying.

Yes, I know you are praying. I am answering.

Please...... I am praying. Our father who is in heaven

You are at it again, calling me, well here I am.

But I do not mean anything by that. I was just, you know what I mean, saying my prayers. I say that same prayer every day. I feel better having said it. It always seems like a good way to start the day. Say the prayer get it out the way and get on with the day.

Then please continue.

Honoured be your name.

Hold on just a second. What do you mean by that?

By what?

Honoured be your name.

I mean...... I mean. What exactly do I mean? I am not so sure now that you put me on the spot and ask me. To be really honest I have never given that much thought before. It is just there the second line of the prayer What does it mean anyway?

It means that you will respect and give a special place to my name in your daily life and dealing.

Yes, that makes some sense. I can see that now that you explain it to me. it is a strange way to speak about another so it does not come easily.

Honoured be your name. Your Kingdom come. Your will be done on earth as it is in heaven.

HOLD IT! Do you really mean all of that?

Of course, why would I not?

Then please tell me what it is you are doing to make that happen?

DOING? DOING? I am doing nothing. I just thought it would be nice if we now and again had a bit of heaven down here now and again. if maybe you took a bit more control once in a while.

Do I have any control over your life?

Well, I attend church almost every Sunday.

Ah but that was not what I asked you. I look at your life and I see that I have not really got much of an influence in the things that you say and do. Most of what you earn you spend on yourself. You seem to have a fair number of habits that do not seem to fit with my having much control over your actions.

Hold on a second, please. You seem to be picking on me. What about all those other hypocrites that I see in the church every Sunday?

Excuse me. I thought this was your prayer. I thought this was about your life. I thought this was about my will being done in your daily life? If that is to happen then it has to begin with you and your relationship with me, never mind the others, that is between them and me.

Yes, I suppose you are correct. I have some bad habits that is certainly true. Things I would be much better without. Some things spring easily to mind and I am sure if I stopped and thought I would be able to come up with a few others that I would be all the better for being rid of. I am sure you have spotted even more.

YES, I have.

I had not really given it much thought if I am being completely honest. There are some things in my life that I continue to do often in spite of promising that I would not do so again. Some things I just keep on doing, and I would be much better if I did not.

That sounds better, now we seem to be getting somewhere. Together we might just manage to make some changes. This sounds positive.

Look, God, I have loads to do today, do you think we could get this prayer over with? Can I please continue? Give us our daily bread.

Now, while we are on that subject. Do you not think that maybe a bit less in the way of eating might do you a bit of good? There might also be a bit more for those who could really do with it.

Please, just a minute. What is this? Is this criticise me day? Here I was doing my religious duty for the day and what happens I find I am being questioned about my actions and my lifestyle.

Praying is a dangerous business you should know that. If you pray and mean it some things might in fact change. You might actually find demands are being made of you. You ask me things. I listen. Then I answer. That can be dangerous. Let us continue.

I am getting a bit wary of continuing.

Wary of what? What are you afraid of?

The next line, that is what I am wary of. I know what is coming next.

Well, let us continue.

Forgive us our sins

What about Robert.

I knew this was going to happen. I had a feeling the minute I said that his name would crop up. He was as much to blame as I was, for that difference and break up we had. I was hurt also in that event.

But what about your prayer/

I did not really mean that.

102

At least you are being honest for once. But it cannot be at all easy carrying all that anger around with you all the time. All that bad feeling and hatred must be causing you some anxiety?

It is not easy. I am sure I will feel better once I have had the opportunity to even the score. When I get my own back. What was it that somebody said, "Do not get angry, get your own back?" I have many plans to do just that. He will be wishing he had never met me when I am finished with him.

You will not feel one little bit better. The truth is if you do as you say you will probably end up feeling even worse than you do now. If you let me I can change all of that right this minute.

You can? How can you do that?

Forgive Robert. In that instant, I, in turn, will forgive you.

NO! I cannot, can I? Yes, I could. I will forgive him this very minute and when I am finished I will convey that to him. Even as I say that I am aware that he is probably feeling every bit as bad as I have been.

How does that feel? To have forgiven him.

I feel good. So much better than I did before I began this prayer earlier. Truth to be told I already feel better than I have in a very long time. Yes, I feel good.

You have not finished your prayer, please let us continue.

Lead us not into temptation but deliver us from evil.

Yes. That is good I will do exactly what you ask. Remember though it is so much easier if you do not put yourself in the way of temptation.

 Please explain just what you mean by that?

You know exactly what I mean. I mean to keep away from the things that you know you find tempting that every time you give in to the temptation you always feel so much worse because you have given in. I can and will help. But remember I am neither your escape hatch or your crutch.

Again, please explain.

You frequently get yourself into trouble. Often when you do you turn to me. You frequently make promises. If I help you out of this you promise never to do such and such again. Or you say that if I help you this time you promise to do so many things. Promises made but seldom kept.

Yes, I remember. I am aware of the promises I made but when things turned out for the better, I did not link that to an answered prayer. I put it down to good fortune.

Well, maybe you will remember in future. Please complete your prayer.

For yours be the power and the glory.

So it will be. if you just remember this prayer and this conversation. If you stop just reciting it but begin to listen to and heed the words. Together we just might begin to make a difference.

AMEN. Thanks be to you.

Christmas Child -Easter Man

When life is full of questions,
and no answers can be found.
When clouds seem dark and black,
despair is all around.
When the road ahead seems frightening.
Each day is hard to bear.
We can feel so lost and helpless,
with not a soul to care.
If we turn our eyes from the moment,
from the day
to find the child of Christmas,
as he lies amidst the hay.
We can see the Man of Easter
and the horrors of the cross.
Then we know he hears our calling,
our every single loss.
For the Christmas Child is near us
we do not stand alone.
Not only at this season
is he here to take our hand.
Each day throughout the year.
He travels there beside us,
in all things, with us, he takes his stand.
So, let the CHILD OF CHRISTMAS
be a gift to you this year.
And have the MAN beside,
throughout the coming year.

Christmas Alone.

"In the beginning, was the Word, and the Word was with God, and the Word was God. He was with God in the beginning. Through him all things were made; without him, nothing was made that was made."
John 1;1-3

Christmas, Easter, Birthdays and Anniversaries; some of the high moments of life. It is so often at these times that we become aware like at no other time of our frailty. These events and moments make us acutely aware of all that happens around us. A wedding anniversary when a spouse is no longer there to be part of the celebration seems like a pit of emptiness. A birthday spent alone can be equally as desolate.

Christmas like no other can be the very worst. We are bombarded from every angle about the message of joy and good tidings. We are reminded not just daily but many times a day that this is the season of goodwill and families.

The deadline for parcels and Christmas card sending is fast approaching. For most people, these positive messages can become reminders of what once was and now how alone you have become.

Cards do not drop through the post with every postal delivery and the thought of preparing a special meal to sit and eat alone can be destroying.

My first ever Christmas after becoming a member of the Christian Church and fellowship was spent away from home. For possibly the first time in my life, I sensed loneliness and aloneness.

I was living in a commune and all the members of the group had gone to stay with family and friends. As I walked home from a midnight service I had attended I was very aware that it was now Christmas day and here I was utterly alone. I knew for certain that I was not the only person who would be full of such thoughts and feelings. For me this was the first of many; it would be one in a string of such empty lonely Christmas days.

There was a Christmas Tree in the flat where we all lived and I sat down in front of it and felt the tears of loneliness run down my cheeks.

I looked at the tree and became very conscious that this symbol of Christmas held all the ingredients of the Cross of Easter. For the first time ever in my fairly short life, I became aware of an inflowing peace and calm. A calm that passes all understanding. The peace of Christmas wrought from the cross of Easter.

To speak of this peace that passes all understanding takes on a real sense meaning only when we are aware of the pain involved in that peace being available to us today. If the wood of the tree speaks of the desolation of the Easter man, then it speaks aloud hallelujah of the joy and comfort of the Christmas Child.

A Good Church Meeting?

I entered the hall,
it was full of mingling people.
Groups of happy smiling cheerful souls.
A man sat at a table and called the meeting to order,
he welcomed me as he had all others.
I felt at home, among friends,
yet strangers.
The chairperson spoke with a genuine fervour
of the aims and purpose of their being there.
Others spoke of how they had been brought
from dark to light.
Each one then another,
told of the Good News.
How far they had fallen,
but now they were back and the way ahead looked good.
I spoke as I had so oft before.
Aware of the love that filled the room.
I was uplifted,
I was refreshed and renewed.
I left that hall as if soaring on the wings of eagles.
A new purpose in each stride.
Oh, that every meeting was just like this,
How glad I was that I was there.
Yet tinged was my heart,
for this was not a meeting of a church,
not a Christian gathering as such.
For I was there that night as a guest
of Alcoholics Anonymous.
I had learned much as I tarried in their midst.
For here I saw the Love of Christ
as seldom had before.
Like no church I had ever known
had ever shown.
Had a leper entered there that night
a welcome they would find.
No questions would be asked,
of why they came or who they were.
As at a good church meeting

A Good Meeting

"My brothers, as believers in our glorious Lord Jesus Christ, don't show favouritism. Suppose a man comes into your meeting wearing a gold ring and fine clothes, and a poor man in shabby clothes also comes in. If you show special attention to the man wearing the fine clothes and say, "here is a good seat for you, " but say to the poor man, "You stand here," "or sit on the floor at my feet," have you not discriminated among yourselves and become judges with evil thoughts?"

James 2: 1-4

While on holiday one summer I took time on a Saturday evening to discover where the nearest church was and to read the noticeboard to find the times of the services the next day. I was pleased to discover that the church closest to the caravan site I was staying on had two services the next day. One was to be held at the normal time held every Sunday of the year, but there was also to be an earlier one. It was mentioned that this was to try and accommodate holidaymakers who might wish to make the best of their day. It sounded to me that I had found an interesting and seemingly friendly congregation making arrangements to be helpful for visitors.

I decided there and then that I would attend the early service at 9-30 am. I arrived at the church in plenty of time and on entering I said good morning to those on duty at the door. They were there to be the welcoming face of the church and to make sure I had a hymn book for the service. I got what could only be described as some rather grumbled good mornings. Nobody asked if I was a visitor to the area? Had I worshipped there before? Maybe I was new to the area and a possible future member of their congregation, but nobody had time to find out. A sullen good morning, then back to the conversation I had interrupted.

I entered the church itself and found myself a seat. As I sat down, I turned to say good morning to the person sitting just a little further along the pew. Just as I was about to speak the owner of the head turned it away from my direction.

The minster came into the church and before the service itself began, he announced that there would be coffee after the service, in the side hall. After the service, I went to the hall and purchased a coffee and waited for some conversation. It did not happen; I was left standing and the various groups who obviously were regular members spoke among themselves. I was left alone. I, left alone without a single person even taking the time to acknowledge my existence.

I returned to my car ready to head off back to my caravan and family. In the glove compartment of my car I had a clerical shirt and clerical collar. I had conducted a funeral service just before leaving to come on holiday and had placed it there and changed into summer attire.

I decided to put it on and return to the church for the later service. This time I was greeted at the door like a long-lost friend. I did not have to even say good morning. When I sat in the pew I had sat in earlier a man sitting further along moved closer and began to speak with me, as did the person sitting in the seat in front of me.

Now possibly on my earlier visit, I had just had a very bad experience and not the normal, but I suspected not. I was certain that the fact I was now wearing a clerical collar had made a vast difference.

I have visited churches where the response had been the very opposite to my earlier experience, but sadly not very often and what I had witnessed and experienced earlier was sadly the norm.

I have been at gatherings and services so often where I have been made to feel like an alien from a different planet. My poem above tells of another meeting where I had been invited to be a guest speaker. I was very conscious of the fact that at this meeting every person who entered the hall was treated like everybody else. It mattered not what they were wearing. Each individual was treated with the greatest respect and made to feel welcome and wanted. Total strangers were very quickly introduced to others and instantly accepted as part of the group.

We must if we are to take the hand of the man from Galilee, learn that we have to take the hand of the person that has found themselves in our midst. It must matter not what the hand looks like. It matters not the colour of the hand or its cleanliness. This person has been put in our midst and we must react as Jesus himself would have in that same situation.

Alone

Alone I wandered.
White capped sentinels high towering.
Through the valley of the shadow.
I meandered.
Mystic majesty.
Creation of wonder.
Around and near,
yet feel no fear.
Light of the sky,
light of life.
Light and Life for me
majestic beauty.
Behold the beholder.
Small I may be.
But here I see.
A hand in all.
In Me;
As I am part,
at one.
Creation and Me.

The Lord is My Shepherd

The Lord is my shepherd;
I have everything I need.
He lets me rest in the fields of green grass,
and leads me beside quiet pools of fresh water.
He gives me strength.
He guides and leads me on true paths,
as he promised.
Even though I go through the deepest darkness.
I will not be afraid, Lord.
For you are with me,
where all my enemies can see me;
You welcome me as an honoured guest,
and fill my cup to the brim.
I know your goodness and love
will be with me all my life.
And your house will be my home
as long as I shall live.

Psalm 23.

I remember walking one day in the Ochil Hills in Scotland in the middle of winter. I was meandering, or as we Scottish say, I was stravaiging through a deep valley. The hills on either side were steep and capped with snow. I was following the course of a stream as it wound its way down to join, and become part of, the River Forth.

The depth of the valley made me very conscious of my stature. As I wandered the clouds began to darken and look threatening. For a moment I felt very alone.

How easily this place could become a frightening place to be, how easy for it to become, "the valley of the shadow of death.' yet I did not feel afraid that day. Neither did I feel alone. The very opposite was the case, I felt very much at one with everything around me.

I realised I was very much a part of all of this, wonderful creation. For that moment I felt very aware of being in this place for a reason. I felt as though I was meant to be there at that point in time at this moment. I was here to experience this frightening beauty, and to know I was not alone.

I heard in my inner being the words of Psalm twenty-three. I heard the line, "Even if I go through the valley of deepest darkness, I will not be afraid."

Those words in this setting brought a deep sense of the meaning of the words. They became more than just words on a sheet or in a book, they became living and real. I did not feel alone; it was as if I did indeed have a guarding shepherd.

I became aware that day, that life has indeed many frightening moments and times. But even in such moments, we need not fear. That because of this even death itself has no sting. We are in life never alone. We are ever surrounded by God or as others say, Chi. To be at one with creation removes fear.

The Rich Young Man.

I was raised in a very strict family home. My father was a very religious man, and a regular attendee of the synagogue, he made sure that I also attended and paid attention to what was happening and what was being said. So I learned from the teachers of the law.

As I grew older I frequently became involved in the synagogue discussions and helped my own in many of the religious debates. In truth, it was often the case that I more than held my own; I frequently came out on top of the debate. I did enjoy debating with the elders of the synagogue.

As I grew older the things of the synagogue became less important. What I was really looking for was how to find the way of life that would bring me happiness. I wanted," the good life." I still made sure that I kept the commandments, I observed all the holy days and festivals and I made all the sacrifices expected of a young man like myself. I often did that little bit more than was expected of me, so I lived my life fulfilling the laws of the synagogue and yet seeking to find the way that would bring me more.

All of this I did and yet I kept asking myself what was it that was missing from my life? Why was I not happy? I felt unsettled and seldom content and kept asking myself what was it that I was looking for? Something was missing, something that I just could not put my finger on.

I was well off financially, I had all and more than a young man of my age could expect to have. In reality, I was better off than a great many of my peers. I had a good job, I had servants who did all the things that we would rather not have to do ourselves. Why then was I not content and happy with my lot? What was it that was eating away inside me making me feel restless?

It was while I was doing all this inner searching and asking myself all these questions that I began to hear talk of a man named Jesus. I heard exciting rumours about this man, people seemed to be stirred by his words. He was preaching and debating with people about seeking and finding the Kingdom of God.

The more I heard about this man the more I felt convinced that this seemed to speak to my inner yearnings. There was something about his talking of having a true relationship with God that stirred me. I found myself asking if I did, in fact, have any real relationship with Him? This man Jesus seemed to be saying that it was possible to have a life full of religion and yet not know God. He spoke as if there was a quality of knowing. There was a difference between knowing about God and actually knowing God.

This seemed to be very much in harmony with the thoughts I had been having. I found myself more and more plagued with the question: Did I know God, did I really know him?

Another thing I heard that he spoke about was inheriting Eternal Life. That certainly took hold of my inner thinking, here was somebody speaking about some of the deeper more meaningful questions that often filled my thinking. This I wanted to hear more about. He was talking about life, and more than life, this was indeed radical thinking.

I made up my mind that I had to seek out this man and speak with him. So I set about finding out where he was and where I could make sure I had the opportunity to speak with him. This was not difficult, he was after all the talk on everybody's lips.

Finding him was, as I suspected not at all difficult, but finding an opportunity to talk with him was not so easy. He was constantly surrounded by people.

After a few attempts, I managed to find myself near the front of the crowd, helped by my obvious wealth and fine dress. "What do I have to do to inherit this Eternal Life you speak of?" I asked him. I had found an opportunity to speak with him and I was not going to waste it talking small talk- get in there with the important questions- do not waste this chance, I thought.

I was taken aback. He was having none of my superior attitudes. Without answering me he began to question me about my life. What did I know about God and religion?

I left him in no doubt. I told him that I kept all the laws of God, that I attend synagogue worship regularly, that I did all that was expected of me and a little bit more.

Then came the ridiculous. "Then sell what you have and give it to the poor," he said. "Then come and follow me."

You have to be joking I thought. Sell all I had, and give it all away. Give away all I possessed? This man must be mad. Whoever heard such stupid ideas and suggestions? It was God who had given me all that I possessed so why would I want, or why would he want me to give it all away. I reasoned that God had given me all of this because I was a good and righteous person.

Why should I contemplate for one moment giving away all I had? I was certain of one thing, such talk was nonsense. This man had got it all wrong. Give away all I have? Such talk was utter nonsense indeed.

So I turned and left. As I walked away I expected him to follow after me. He had spoken of joining him and following him, he realised that I would indeed be a good catch, a good person to be part of his band of followers. There would not be many with the wealth that I had who wanted to do right by their religion, he was sure to come after me he would not wish to lose me.

No, he did not come after me, he left me to walk away. Twice I wondered if I should return and give him a second opportunity to change his mind and accept me as I was. Deep down inside as I walked away from him I knew I was deluding myself. This man was not going to come after me, he had spoken his mind and was not going to change it.

I could see that and that this was going to be no more than one of those little episodes in my life.

Yet I still to this day feel that there is something sadly wrong with my life. My religion does not bring any sense of contentment that seems to be with those who follow, "The Way," seem to have. That is what they are now calling the followers of this man Jesus, followers of the way. They, unlike me, seem to have found a feeling of inner peace and a real sense of contentment. I still do not have that courage required to give myself to follow him. I am tempted but afraid to make the decision.

It is the case that if we desire to find meaningful life and purpose in our lives it will not come free. Sacrifice has to be made. It frequently means letting go of some of the things that stop you from finding that inner peace and calm. It is no simple matter to put your trust in a belief or an idea if it means letting go of the things in life held dear.

The Woman Who Touched His Cloak

Can you imagine for just one moment what it is like to be classed as unclean, as an untouchable, a person to be avoided? Then let me tell you just exactly what it is like. It is in no way something that could ever be called fun. To watch people who once spoke to you cross the street to avoid you. To be aware that the market traders will not look you in the eye or touch you when you reach out to take your purchases. They make very sure there will be no physical contact between you and them.

I can tell you how terrible it is when your family keep themselves well out of contact with you, it hurts deep in the heart. How I longed for the touch of a human hand, to be held by my husband, to touch my children's cheeks. It is like living each day in your own little hell.

There was just no solution anywhere. It is not possible to pack up and go anywhere else because it would be just the same there. Then of course, I was bound to the family, bound to my religion. To move to another town would only impound my problems, then I would be totally isolated and there would be not one person who even cared.

So I am sure you can imagine how I felt that day when I heard that the man Jesus was not far from town and was heading our way. I had heard so much about him, the things he was saying and the things that happened in his presence. I wondered that day if there could be a help for me if I could just get close enough to him. I was sure that if I could just speak to him that his words would be a great help and comfort to me. I had heard all kinds of reports; people who had been helped to walk, those helped to see, the tales went on.

I just had this feeling that although I had suffered all those twelve years he would be able to lift this heartache from me. There were others who had been lying on their beds for longer than me who had found help.

118

That night I could not sleep at all. I tossed and turned all night long as I thought of the next day and the possibilities it might hold for me. The next day came and I arose full of excitement I had never felt before. I wanted to be out there awaiting his arrival. Each hour seemed like a day and each minute like an hour as I waited. I could think of nothing else.

Then there was a crowd of people and the word was moving around them that he was on his way. I looked and there in the distance, I could see him surrounded by people. How was I ever going to get anywhere near him, so many people? My heart began to sink my hopes began to dissipate.

I knew that I must not come into contact with him, I was unclean. Somehow though I had to be able to speak with him, he was my last and only hope.

Just as he drew near, I saw a gap appear a way open up before me. I was going to get my opportunity to just speak with him. Just at the very moment, I moved forward a well-dressed person of high rank stepped in front of me. He was one of the ruling class, I was a mere untouchable.

He spoke to Jesus. I saw the pain in his eyes as he did so. He was telling Jesus of his daughter who had been so ill he was sure she was on her death bed. He was asking Jesus to go and lay his hands on her that she might have a life again.

His need was far greater than mine, of this I was certain. More importantly, there was a child who had a life before her. Her life was like a candle that was being snuffed out and her only a child. True, my life was not all that I had hoped for but at least I still had a life. This small child it seemed was losing even that. As I watched and listened I could see and feel the pain of this family. How could I possibly detract Jesus from this man and his needs? They were greater than mine ever would be.

I stepped aside and watched as he walked past me with the grieving ruler. My heart went out to him and I prayed that Jesus would indeed be able to help him.

Then, like a bolt from out the of blue, it came to me, like a blinding light. I do not need to speak to him, I do not need to detract him from what is much more important. The task at hand for him and the ruler is much more important than mine.

If I can just lay one finger on his cloak, even just the hem of his cloak would be enough. I was convinced this was all it would take. One touch, one small touch on the hem of his cloak, this was all I needed. Never before in life had I felt anything as certainly as this.

I moved forward; I reached out; only one or two centimetres was all it would take. I hesitated, was I about to break all the rules? Was I about to call live coals onto my head? NO, I felt sure it would be fine. I reached out once more and this time I felt my fingers just brush off the hem of his robe.

It was an amazing feeling. I felt life flow through me touching every single part of me, every fibre of my being. I felt well like I had not felt for years. I could reach out and touch others because of this fleeting touch of the cloak of this man, this Jesus.

I had thought it was time to just slip into the background. To return and show myself to the chief priest and return to my family. How I longed to see them, to touch them, to hold them.

It was not to be so simple. Jesus turned and I saw those penetrating eyes looking at me and through me. I felt a moment of panic, but his eyes were full of encouragement. "Take heart, my daughter," he said. "Your faith has this day made you clean." So calmly he accepted what had happened, what he had done for me. So lovingly he sent me on my way.

What about the little girl? She was restored to full life. Sounds all so very simple, and so it was. Two families rejoiced that day. Two families had experienced a resurrection.

The briefest touch of another can often change the lives of those who seek and are in need. To be touched at the very core of your being can change and restore us. So reach out your hand, stretch forth your heart that they may be touched like touching the hem of His cloak. For life can be changed in a fleeting moment if the mind is open and ready to receive.

I remember (No More)

I watch the drops of rain run down the window pane,
small rivers following their unmapped course.
I have watched this window day after day
for long and weary months.
I saw the man with the mower in the summer sun,
and remembered stacks of grass we jumped into and threw at
each other.
I remember other things we threw,
like the stones against the glass.
I hear the sound, and feel the fear
of being caught.
Running until breathless, hiding.
I have watched the falling leaves
from trees of gold and brown.
Watched as the last one held on.
Willing it to stay for me.
I remember the rustle and noise of fallen leaves,
kicked underfoot with a joyful sound.
Through this "pain,' this pane
I have monitored the days gone by and seasons change.
Summer to autumn,
to this the winter of my life.
I remember sledging children,
laughing, cold, yet full of fun.
No more these things of life for me.
No more to lie and hold my husband fast.
No more the sounds of summer joys,
or children's hugs.
No more, for life is swiftly moving on.
But, no more do I fear
tomorrow or the next.
For through this pain.
I have caught a glimpse of Him.
I have seen beyond tomorrow,
and today's deep sorrow,
to the gates of life eternal.

My heart has heard a whispered voice.
That speaks of more to be.
For even death cannot divide.
All that is bound with He.

The above poem was written after speaking with a young mother of two children, dying of cancer in a hospice room. Also, another two friends, Kate and Sandy, who I was with as they parted this world. All three I felt privileged to be with through this time and they touched me in so many ways.

Fear of the Unknown

"Do not let your hearts be troubled; trust in God and trust also in me. In my Father's house, there are many rooms; if it were not so I would have told you. I go to prepare a place for you, I will come back and take you with me, that you also may be where I am."

John 14: 1-3

Over the years I had listened to a great many ministers declaring that they had no fear of death. They held absolutely no fear at all within them of the prospect of life coming to an end.

On the other hand, had to be honest with myself and my friends that I was envious of such people because this was not my experience. Sadly, I was not so honest with members of my congregations, for like others, I said that death held no fear. I must have sounded convincing because in all my years as a minister, or at any other times, had anybody questioned my sincerity.

That being said, I always had a deep and nagging suspicion that I was not removing any fears from anybody. I suspected I was preaching a hollow message; I certainly did not feel full of courage in the knowledge of the inevitable.

I could never, though, put my finger on what it was that I feared, what it was I was afraid of. I had been with a great many people as they died, and it did not seem at all frightening. In fact, I cannot remember a single person whose death did not seem a release. A release from frailty or pain.

I had this recurring thought in my wakeful nights that I wanted to watch my children grow and mature and become settled. I did not want to leave them. Whatever it was, I was afraid of death and because of this fear, I often felt a hollow feeling in speaking the words of resurrection and life after death. I discussed this with fellow ministers and every time I left feeling worse and wishing I had not raised the issue.

Then I met this young woman dying from cancer, the word we seem afraid to speak of. We spoke together and shared our thoughts and fears and together somehow, we began to find fears disappear. As we shared, her fear seemed to disappear and with hers so mine.

The experience changed the rest of my ministry. It led to other similar experiences and encounters and I was no longer wary of speaking with those facing death. Once such a person, the mother of a very dear friend and a member of my congregation, strengthened my experiences as she shared her feelings, her illness and her dying with me. A dear elder of my last church asked me to be with him as he died. Between these three wonderful people, my fear of death and dying was lifted.

So much is lost when we play games in the midst of death. Pretending it is not happening, or that we have a faith that is not real. Such moments are too precious to pretend. Those three, and many others since have assured me that death is not something to fear but to face. They still speak to me and have done so over the years and in so doing live on in my life.

Poppies

I was feeling low,
in dark despair.
Caught in a time warp of my own,
a black and lonely abyss.
Not a thought beyond my own.
No cares beyond the cares of selfish me.
Poor little me.
Why is life so cruel? I asked.

The beating drum of ME, ME, ME
and MY, MY, MY.
Drowned every sound
except the hammering noise within my head.

Then there before me,
blood red in all their glory
stood a field of poppies.
Their vibrant hues pulled me from my pit.
Back into the world of wonderful creation.
I thought of years of blood,
poured forth for such as me.
Wars fought by man,
that I might have this day.
Free to wander the paths of life.
There before me,
blood red in all their glory
stood a field of poppies.
I thought of Him,
who emptied out his life.
I heard birds sing,
around the beauty I did see.
No more the thoughts of ME.
Then, in the sound of silence,
I heard a voice.
And drank the deep refreshing joy of life,
with thankful heart.
How precious is each beating moment?
And won at such a cost.

I can do what I want with my life.

How often over the years have you heard words such as those, "I can do what I want with my life. It is mine, and you cannot tell me what to do."

I can remember uttering these very words as a teenager on more than one occasion. At that age, we can almost be forgiven for not fully understanding the sacrifices that had been made on our behalf or the concern that parents and family had for our welfare.

The trouble is that many never grow out of those selfish ways of thinking, we cling to our thoughtless attitudes. This present age in which we live almost positively encourages us to think this way. We are encouraged to do our own thing, to think first and foremost of number one, self-centeredness is the mode of the day.

Maybe once we have made it in life, become successful, become a great entrepreneur, we can look back and let our wealth trickle down to those less fortunate.

Such selfish thinking can only, and has, led to a divided society in which the poor get poorer and the rich increase in wealth owning. Around us, we only have to look to see the increasing broken relationships and families. Society itself becomes torn asunder.

The deeper such thinking eats into society the more the younger generation look around them and wonder what life has in store for them.

It is not only at the level of society that damage is done. Such selfish thinking is far from good for the individual. It frequently, and more often leads to loneliness and in turn despair. Another consequence of such thinking is the increase in those who think that they should always get what they desire. All desires should be fulfilled. Many even believe that it is the right of being here, society owes us a living.

We can see those who, when they do not get exactly what it is they want and when they want it, throw a tantrum.

How many times during my ministry I came across people who had left the fellowship of the church because the minister had said something they did not like to hear. "I am not listening to that," they say and off they head. Some to another church but many more to the womb of their own thinking and living.

Sadly, even within the bounds of religion, it becomes little more than a pick and mix of comfortable ideas with a personal faith challenged by nobody.

How much time is spoiled quietly walking the paths of resentment, building up new and better ways to, "get my own back."

One day I saw a field of poppies, so unexpected and magnificent. It lifted me from selfish thoughts of myself to the many sacrifices that had been made on my behalf. If this was true for me it is equally true for us all. Nobody is an island.

It is worthwhile, from time to time, stopping and considering the many who have made sacrifices for us even when we did not ask for such. To consider and rejoice that they have. As a society, we need to ask ourselves if we are being true to all of those who have gone before and given much, often their lives, that we might have ours.

The Healing of the Deaf and Mute Man

Life before the day I am speaking of had always been very difficult. Have you ever attempted to tell somebody something important without the ability to use words? Some of the children of Decapolis played a game where they tried to do just that, but for me, this had been no game.

I had to live all my life up until this point doing just that trying very hard to help them to understand what it was I was trying to say. They also had difficulty, they did want to understand me and make me a part of the group and conversation, but they so often struggled to make out what it was I was trying to convey to them.

I could not hear, I could not speak and I had a head full of ideas that I so desperately wanted to share with others.

How often I felt so alone because others had given up on me or they were too embarrassed to be seen in my company. Then there were those times when somebody had given me time and shown a great deal of patience, yet I ended up frustrated, unable to convey to the person those inner thoughts. Then came the anger; this was by far the worst. It was also self-defeating, the angrier I got, the worse it became.

To be really honest it was amazing I had any friends at all. Yet I did. Friends who in spite of all things continued to show me patience, even when I least deserved it; friends who tolerated the anger and time after time made allowances for my behaviour. Friends who once they managed to understand what it was I was trying to convey became very understanding and helpful. How grateful I was that they had stayed around all those years.

A few days ago they came to me and spoke to me about a man, a man by the name of Jesus. He was going to be in the region not far from where we lived. They felt that he could possibly help me and my situation. They were trying very hard to convince me that it might be worth my time going and trying to meet him. After all, what had I to lose?

My first reaction was to say no, something I never found any problem conveying, a simple shake of the head was all it took. I was aware that such a reaction would result in a long and difficult attempt to explain my reasons for not wishing to give it a try. They seemed enthusiastic about this idea and I became aware that saying no to could lose me the only friends I had. They seemed so certain that this man, Jesus, would be able to help me.

It seemed a shame to disappoint them with a simple shake of the head, to take away a very genuine desire to help me. It could indeed do no harm. What else was I going to do anyway? There was very little I could do, except beg on the street corner.

So we set off to go and try to meet with this man Jesus, the man from Nazareth. As we travelled the road it became very obvious that we were not the only ones with the idea of meeting and listening to him. Everybody seemed to be heading in the same direction as us. There seemed to be only one thing on the minds of the many, to meet with Jesus. He really was a crowd puller.

When, after travelling in the hot sun, we eventually arrived, he was surrounded by a great many people. There was a real feeling of excitement in the air, even though I could not hear it I could sense it.

My friends were not the sort of people to be deterred in any way. They began to push their way through the crowd pulling me along behind them. I could not hear what was being said to them, but I could see in their eyes that there was much anger in the air, I was familiar with this.

Eventually, we stood in front of him, the man Jesus; he was looking at me and I at him. It became very obvious to me very quickly that this was no ordinary man. being unable to hear or speak I had learned to develop the use of the other senses I had. I had learned to read what people were like, I was able to see beyond the outer person and discern the quality of the inner being. What I saw when I looked at this man intrigued me.

I saw my friends take hold of his arm and pull them closer so that they would be heard above the crowd. Of course, I could not hear what was being said, I could almost lip read the odd little bit, but I would be lying if I said I fully understood. What they were saying was something about putting hands on me. I was not sure what they meant by that.

The next thing I knew was that his hand was on my shoulder and he was taking me away from my friends and the crowd. His followers stepped between us and the crowd instructing them to stand still and wait. He gently led me to a side street, I wondered what this was all about.

Once we were far enough away I felt his finger touching my ears, those useless organs. My first thought was, please do not hurt me, my second almost instant thought was to wonder if I had cleaned my ears that morning? It is strange what goes through the mind when you feel unsure of just what is happening to you.

Then I watched as he spat on his fingers, so much for me wondering about cleanliness. He reached towards my mouth, which I am sure was wide open in awe. "What was all this about?"

I watched as he put his fingers towards my mouth and then I felt the touch of his finger on my tongue. He looked skywards and sighed, he said, "Ephphatha." I knew that this meant, be opened.

Then it dawned on me, I had just heard him say that word, I had heard him say it. No doubt about it I had heard the word, Ephphatha.

I had heard, I could hear. I said, "Thank you." it did not for one-second express what I wanted to say but I could not find any other words. Then the reality hit me, I had thanked him, the words, only two of them but they had been spoken by me. I was ecstatic.

Then I became aware of the sounds of all the people not far from us. How thoughtful Jesus had been, he had taken me aside from the crowd to protect me from a terrible inrush of sound. Such would have been far too much for one who had never before heard a sound, never mind a noise like I was hearing faintly.

Then my friends were there beside me. I spoke to them, "Shalom." I saw the amazement in their eyes and on their faces. They began jumping up and down holding each other almost dancing with excitement. They were excited, I was excited.

Once more I felt that strong yet gentle hand on my shoulder; it was the hand of Jesus. He asked us to leave, but in an insistent way told us to say nothing to anybody. Speak to nobody about what had happened down that side street. I could speak. I could hear. Tears were flowing done my face, how could I possibly not tell everybody about what had just happened? Never! I want to shout from the rooftops of every home between here and my own house. I wanted the world to know.

When Jesus opens the ears of the deaf, they hear of his love. When the mouths of the dumb are opened they only wish to sing praise. Those who do not wish to hear good news or sing for joy have not begun to understand the joy of the Word. For once you begin to understand the Word even the stones would shout praise.

The Last Supper

You enter an upstairs room having climbed a narrow staircase. The room has bare white walls, and at the far end, there stands a table that has obviously been made ready for a meal. From what appears on the table it is clear that the meal that is to be celebrated is the Passover. The two things that give you this is the presence of a boiled egg that has been blackened by being held over a smoking candleflame, the other is the unleavened bread.

Around the table, you see reclined on cushions the twelve followers of Jesus. Sitting in the centre spot is Jesus. There is a feeling of expectancy in the room, mixed with the general feeling that comes with the celebration of the Passover. The Passover holds a very important place in the lives of the Jewish community, they are to celebrate it with their master and Friend. The joyful feeling is only slightly incomplete, in as much as some of the followers of Jesus are not fully aware of the depth of what had happened as they entered the room between Jesus and Mary Magdalene and a jar of very precious ointment.

There is though, in spite of this, a real air of anticipation, and joy.

You are part of this, allow that feeling of expectancy and joy that is in the room to flow into your being..............

The last of the celebration meal is being brought to the table by the women who had been in the upper room for some time prior to the arrival of Jesus and his disciples, preparing the meal.

You are invited to take a seat at the table and do so, trying hard to not be too noticeable..........

The disciples are all talking about the years they have spent with Jesus travelling around the country, slowly but surely heading towards Jerusalem, where they have now reached. You let the words sink into your mind.............

The meal begins and Jesus reaches over to the unleavened bread. You watch as he raises it to the level of his chin..............

He breaks it in half,,,,,,,,,,,,,,,, He looks around the table making eye contact with each person present...............

Your eyes and his meet.............

You expect to hear some of the words recited at the Passover but instead, in a quiet voice Jesus says, "This is my body broken for you." ...... For you.............

You let these words sink in.......... What is Jesus speaking of? What does he mean by saying his body is broken for them?

There has been much talk of the danger of them entering Jerusalem. Is Jesus speaking of the possibility of his death at the hands of the Romans?

If so this means this bread represents the body of Jesus....... If it is broken for you as he says does this mean that if he dies that you might find something? The forgiveness he spoke of often????????

The bread is passed around the table each present takes a piece and eats it including the women...........

The meal progresses, quieter now as those present consider what has just happened............

Again Jesus reaches over the table, he this time picks up a large tankard of wine. He lifts his eyes again and once more your eyes meet his.

You hear him speak again, this time he says, "This wine is my blood shed for you."............

There is no doubt now what he is meaning. Jesus is most certainly going to die and he is saying he is doing it for all who are gathered, for you...........

There is a deathly hush around the upper room. Everybody present is letting these words sink into their thoughts.........

"This is my body............. This is my blood."............

There is little doubt, Jesus is aware that he will die here in Jerusalem, and his death will have a deep meaning.............

Allow that to sink into your inner being. This man Jesus has walked into a certain trap and death will be inevitable and he has done so knowingly................. For you...........

You watch, him and the disciples........... There is a very close bond among them......... They do not wish to lose him, he does not want to leave them, but he will............

He is telling them he will do so for them............

He is doing it that they and you might live life to the full...............

Past mistakes will be forgotten because they will be forgiven...........

You were given the broken bread, his body broken............. Think of all the things in your life that need forgiveness........... for such his body will be broken.

You have tasted and shared the wine that Jesus said was his blood............. Think of all the things that your fear.......... all the things that hold you back from being what you can and should be.........

For this, his blood was shed......... That you might have life...........

From the hands of Jesus, all have taken the bread and the wine, all have been given the bread and the wine......... Including Judas.

The meal draws to a close..... a very different Passover from expected..........

Judas has left............ he has other things to do...........

Think of all the times you have heard those words repeated. "This is my body broken for you. This is my blood shed for you."

133

How often have they been no more than words? Part of a ceremony. For some, one of the few services of worship they attend and the words mean little.

Remember that this service is part of the church of today. Full of depth and meaning. It still offers freedom from past mistakes and faults. It still offers a new beginning every time the words are repeated. "This is my body broken for You. This is my blood shed for You."

The Crucifixion

You are in the very busy streets of Jerusalem, It is an early Friday morning. it seems to be very much busier and noisier than a normal Friday morning. The crowd sounds angry. Your head is full of the noises of shouting and jeering.............. mocking words can be heard........... fingers are being pointed.

You wonder what exactly is happening. You push your way to the front of this rabble of a crowd.

You see three men, across their shoulders, are large spars of heavy wood. These are the spars that will slot into the upright wood that will make the crosses on which these three men will be nailed and will die.

They are struggling under the weight and it is plain to see that they have been beaten and tortured prior to having to carry these spars. Every so often the three slow their pace and the Roman soldiers who are there take up their whips with their many tails and spikes and lash the backs of the three men. You can hear them as they eat into the flesh, you can almost feel the pain.........

One of the men you recognise to be Jesus, the same Jesus who had ridden into Jerusalem a few days earlier to praise and adulation. As you watch Jesus falls to the ground....... The soldiers lash out telling him to move. He picks himself up and again slowly makes his way forward up the narrow road..............

The crowd follows and you walk alongside Jesus and he toils under the weight.......... No longer do you hear the yelling of the crowd you are caught up in the pain of this man........... Your heart goes out to him.

Again Jesus falls........ again the soldiers beat him about the head and body.......... You so wish you were able to move forward and put a stop to this or offer some help to Jesus.

Slowly they move forward again............

Once more Jesus falls............... This time one of the soldiers turns to a large strong looking man and makes him lift the spar from Jesus' shoulders.........

The procession of men and soldiers with the man now carrying Jesus weight head towards the city gates and pass out through them, you move with them..............

Not far from the gates there is an ugly formed hill, Golgotha..............

They make their way to its summit and the three spars are left to fall to the ground with a clatter............

Two of the soldiers manhandle Jesus roughly throwing him to the ground on top of the large spar that he and the other man have carried to this place.............

From a leather pouch around his waist, one of the soldiers draws out a large-headed iron hammer and three very long nails sharply pointed pieces of metal.........

The first of these pieces of shaped metal is placed to the wrist of Jesus........ his arm is stretched out by the other soldier and the metal is hammered home............. You can hear the shattering of bones as it penetrates......... The soldier keeps hammering making sure the metal is firmly embedded in the wooden spar............

It is difficult to watch...............

The other arm of Jesus is stretched out and the process begins with another metal rod and it is hammered through the wrist of Jesus into the other end of the spar..............

Ropes are secured to both ends of the spar and pulled upwards the body of Jesus hauled up the large standing tree like wood that had been made ready for this act............

It is pulled until it falls into the notch ready to take it. You hear as it falls into place forming the cross on which Jesus will be left to die.............. His feet are crossed and the last of the three metal spikes is driven through his feet and into the triangular bracket that is fitted to the down spar of the cross..........

You watch, and you can feel the tears run down your cheeks as the final crash of the hammer secures his feet..............

The gathered crowd and soldiers jeer and mock, taunting Jesus and the other two............. One of the soldiers yells, "get yourself down from there." ....

A ladder is brought forward and one of the soldiers brings forward a prepared notice. The soldier climbs level to the face of Jesus and nails this notice to the cross above his head. It reads, "Jesus, King of the Jews.".............

Jesus turns and looks to the prisoner on his right-hand side and says to him, "Today you will be with me in Paradise......... This man had spoken some words to Jesus about them deserving to die but him not....................

It begins to rain........... The sky turns black and threatening........ thunder and lightning fill the sky.......

It feels like the middle of the night but it is still only before three o'clock in the afternoon............

In one of the lulls between claps of thunder, Jesus can be heard speaking loudly, *"Eloi Eloi lama sabachthani?"* ....*"My God, My God why have you forsaken me?"*

You watch with a heavy heart...............

Again Jesus calls out........ "Father forgive them, they know not what they do"....................

You feel something very meaningful touch the inner depths of your being as you hear these words.........

You move a little closer to the cross....... your eyes are held by his eyes, even in all of this agony and horror there is a feeling of love and caring............

You stop............ you look up into the eyes of Jesus............

Jesus speaks to you..............

You become aware of many of the past errors and faults of your life, but you are aware of a deep feeling that this is now in the past forgotten and forgiven..........

Jesus calls out one last time, it is three o'clock........... he says," Tetelestai*", "It is finished."*

Finally, he calls out, *"o patéras sta chéria sas diaprátto to pnévma mou" "Father into your hands I commit my spirit."*

Slowly you turn and walk away, not as you would have expected with a heavy heart, but in a real sense of having witnessed something very special happening. You have a sense of having been freed from all past sins and errors.

Give Thanks

A Walk to Emmaus

It is a warm day as you travel along a dusty dry road. It is the middle of the day and the noonday sun is at its highest point in the sky. Two others are walking with you. As your feet hit the road the hot dry dust rises and you can taste it on your lips.

The talk is all about the crucifixion, all about the man Jesus, whom they had watched being nailed to the cross. They, like you, had watched as he died and committed his body to his God and Father.

As you walk you are aware of a feeling of despair and deep sadness......... The heat of the day only adds to the feeling of melancholy..........

The two speak of the high hopes they had held of Jesus and how those hopes now seemed dashed and in ruins..........

Think of some of the hopes and the dreams that you have nurtured that had not come to be........... remember how you have felt as you remembered these hopes.................

The two begin to speak of their fears for the future........... what should they do now? ..... would it be safe for them to return to where they had fished and lived?...................

What if the same happens to them as they witnessed happening to Jesus?...............

Think of the things that in the past have made you afraid of the future..........

As you continue along the dusty trail feeling the warmth under your feet you are joined by another, a stranger...........

He joins in the discussion. You tell him of the thoughts the three of you have been having......... You speak of unfulfilled dreams and hopes...........

You speak of your fear and anxieties for tomorrow.............

You continue along the road.......... as evening approaches and the day begins to cool............ one of the disciples suggests that it is time to stop and make rest.......... and eat.

You enter a house at the side of the road. Still, all the talk is about Jerusalem and what happened there in the past three or so days............

The stranger begins to speak again this time he talks of the prophecies about the one called Messiah..........

One of the other two begins to take from the bag strung around his waist, some food and wine.............

As they sit and make ready to eat they quietly think about the day and all the talk............

Again you are aware of some of the fears you have for the future...........

All for sit at the rough table.......... One of them gives a blessing..........

The stranger reaches across the table and takes into his hands some bread......... he breaks it...... as you watch you hear again the words, "This is my body broken for you."

You look at the stranger and for a moment it is Jesus that you see.......

He hands a piece of the broken bread and once more you hear the words, "This is my body broken for you."............

You take the offered bread...... you eat........ and in the stillness, the fears for tomorrow and the future dissipate...........

You pause and consider your life and remember the times when you had felt alone.......... Now you realise that at no time were you ever alone.

The thoughts and fears about tomorrow disappear as you hear that inner voice remind you of the words of Jesus, "Lo I will be with you to the very end."

All your fears leave you, there is no more terror about the morrow. You are ready to face the here and now and to live life in all its fullness..........

You are full of Joy and Peace

Give thanks.

Amen.

So my journey comes to an end, a time of reflection and contemplation has helped me put this together, I hope it helps you to see some things in a new and fresh light.

A Walk to Emmaus

It is a warm day as you travel along a dusty dry road. It is the middle of the day and the noonday sun is at its highest point in the sky. Two others are walking with you. As your feet hit the road the hot dry dust rises and you can taste it on your lips.

The talk is all about the crucifixion, all about the man Jesus, whom they had watched being nailed to the cross. They, like you, had watched as he died and committed his body to his God and Father.

As you walk you are aware of a feeling of despair and deep sadness......... The heat of the day only adds to the feeling of melancholy..........

The two speak of the high hopes they had held of Jesus and how those hopes now seemed dashed and in ruins..........

Think of some of the hopes and the dreams that you have nurtured that had not come to be........... remember how you have felt as you remembered these hopes.................

The two begin to speak of their fears for the future........... what should they do now? ..... would it be safe for them to return to where they had fished and lived?...................

What if the same happens to them as they witnessed happening to Jesus?...............

Think of the things that in the past have made you afraid of the future...........

As you continue along the dusty trail feeling the warmth under your feet you are joined by another, a stranger...........

He joins in the discussion. You tell him of the thoughts the three of you have been having......... You speak of unfulfilled dreams and hopes...........

You speak of your fear and anxieties for tomorrow.............

You continue along the road.......... as evening approaches and the day begins to cool............ one of the disciples suggests that it is time to stop and make rest.......... and eat.

You enter a house at the side of the road. Still, all the talk is about Jerusalem and what happened there in the past three or so days............

The stranger begins to speak again this time he talks of the prophecies about the one called Messiah..........

One of the other two begins to take from the bag strung around his waist, some food and wine.............

As they sit and make ready to eat they quietly think about the day and all the talk............

Again you are aware of some of the fears you have for the future...........

All for sit at the rough table.......... One of them gives a blessing..........

The stranger reaches across the table and takes into his hands some bread......... he breaks it...... as you watch you hear again the words, "This is my body broken for you."

144

You look at the stranger and for a moment it is Jesus that you see.......

He hands a piece of the broken bread and once more you hear the words, "This is my body broken for you."............

You take the offered bread...... you eat........ and in the stillness, the fears for tomorrow and the future dissipate...........

You pause and consider your life and remember the times when you had felt alone.......... Now you realise that at no time were you ever alone.

The thoughts and fears about tomorrow disappear as you hear that inner voice remind you of the words of Jesus, "Lo I will be with you to the very end."

All your fears leave you, there is no more terror about the morrow. You are ready to face the here and now and to live life in all its fullness..........

You are full of Joy and Peace

Give thanks.

Amen.

So, my journey comes to an end, a time of reflection and contemplation has helped me put this together, I hope it helps you to see some things in a new and fresh light.

Acknowledgements

I would like to express my gratitude to a great number of people who over the years encouraged me to produce this work. Those of my three congregations at Motherwell Manse Road Parish Church, Shotts Calderhead Parish Church, as it was known in that day and Clackmannan Parish Church, where it eventually found its way into print. Changes were asked for at that time by publishers, and the project was shelved. I left the Ministry, to go back to University to become a teacher of Philosophy and World Religions.
Over the years, many asked me what had happened to it, and encouraged me to think again, about looking at it once more. I would like to thank them for thinking it was worthy of the time. The friends who took the time to read it as I worked on it and helped to proofread the manuscript and the final copy both know who they are, and I thank you sincerely for your endeavours. This has not been an easy task because it has meant going back and reliving some difficult memories, I thank those who have helped me with this also. This whole work came out of a period where I was unable to speak and did a great deal of hard thinking. There were many who helped me through those days, I thank them. Much of the material helped me through those very difficult times and I hope they encourage those who read them now.

Printed in Poland
by Amazon Fulfillment
Poland Sp. z o.o., Wrocław